William Russo

with Jeffrey Ainis and David Stevenson

A NEW APPROACH

COMPOSING MUSIC

THE UNIVERSITY OF CHICAGO PRESS · Chicago and London

The University of Chicago Press, Chicago 60637
The University of Chicago Press, Ltd., London

© 1983 by William Russo
All rights reserved. Published 1983
University of Chicago Press edition 1988
Printed in the United States of America

97 96 95 94 93 92 91 90 89   5 4 3 2

Library of Congress Cataloging in Publication Data

Russo, William.
  Composing music.

  Reprint. Originally published: Englewood Cliffs,
N.J. : Prentice Hall, c1983.
  Bibliography: p.
  Includes index.
  1. Composition (Music)   I. Title.
MT40.R88 1988   781.6′1   87-30243
ISBN 0-226-73216-9 (pbk.)

Contents

Preface

This book is intended to teach you how to compose music. If you already compose, it will make you more fluent and will help you to expand the ideas and skills you already have. It is not a book *about* music. It is not a book *about* composition. It is a book that requires your *participation*; you will actually begin composing in the first chapter. Knowledge and experience, in other words, are given in one stroke.

Most of the teaching takes place in the form of exercises; in fact, to read this book is to work through the exercises. Each exercise acquaints you with a particular procedure or resource—information that, in most cases, you will use right away to compose a short piece. I have found this method of teaching to be highly effective. Instant application provides you with instant experience. Furthermore, there is absolutely no better way to learn something than to try it yourself.

The focus of this book is on melody, which is the essence of music. Harmony is also emphasized, and you will be able to gain a good understanding of the important relationship between harmony and melody. Most of the harmonic material is limited to major and minor triads, with the exception of the exercises on "magic" chords and non-3rd chords derived from melody.

I have used only those procedures and materials that have proven to be most useful in my classes. Included in these are topics— words and music and popular music as a source—that have not been dealt with in any other book. Some topics such as isomelody, organum, pointillism, and minimalism may not be immediately familiar to you, but it should take you no time to feel comfortable with them; the instructions and guidelines are very clear and easy to understand.

Whom This Book Is for

This book is for anyone and everyone who wants to compose music. The students in my classes have varying backgrounds, goals, and tastes, and they have all been successful with my method of teaching composition—even those who have only a minimal background in music. To begin this book you should know the treble and bass clefs, the C major scale, the rudiments of time signatures and note values, and how to construct intervals. This knowledge is the equivalent of less than a semester in music theory. In some cases a background in piano study will suffice, and in all cases even a slight ability at the piano is helpful, but not necessary.

A unique aspect of this book is that students at any level can benefit by using it; beginners can start at the bottom, and those with more experience can hone the skills they already have. Further, the structure allows students to concentrate on the areas that are applicable to their individual needs. Teachers will find this book especially useful for this reason. *Composing Music* has been used successfully in two-semester courses at Columbia College, Chicago. It worked particularly well because some of the students were instrumentalists and were able to perform the exercises and examples in class.

While *Composing Music* works well for music courses, it is also suited to self-study. The approach and instructions are straightforward, and you can easily work through the book by yourself. You will find that the book provides all the guidance you need.

About the Exercises

When I teach I encourage my students to compose immediately. The exercises are designed in such a way that only a few elements are available at a time. This approach isolates each detail of the composition process so that each one can be more deeply understood.

For example, in Chapter 9 there is an exercise on "magic" chords in which you are given a unique chord and are asked to compose a melody made up exclusively of tones in this chord. You are given an accompaniment, some suggestions on form and shape, and some other simple guidelines. This is your starting point. When you have completed the exercise, you will feel comfortable basing a melody on the tones of an interesting chord and you will have experienced the unifying influence that such a procedure provides. This sort of exercise improves your ability to develop and control material.

As in the preceding example, each exercise provides you with a specific number of resources to work with. The technique of limiting resources is used extensively throughout this book; it is a most useful and effective method for teaching students how to compose. When you are faced with a blank sheet of music paper and no guidelines, it is often difficult to know how to begin. The limitations act as guidelines and give you the initial direction you will need to complete each exercise. By having a restricted number of resources to work with, you will learn to accomplish more and do less. The beginning composer in particular tends to use more chords, rhythms, and tones than are necessary and frequently gets less than successful results. You will be surprised by the mileage you can get from well-chosen guidelines.

Finally, the order of the chapters is sequential, as it is in most books; but in this book the order does not need to be rigidly adhered to, especially in the later chapters. Whatever your background, I encourage you to complete at least the first four chapters in their proper order. Chapter 8, "Accompaniment Procedures," should be completed before you do the chapters that follow it. Chapter 14, on picture music, may be embarked upon at any time with good results.

Materials You Will Need

For the fill-in exercises you will need a good pencil with soft lead (Eberhard Faber Blackwing 602s, though expensive, are excellent) and a good eraser (the white, plastic type gives very clean results). You will need manuscript paper with a hard surface for the out-of-book projects. I recommend Aztec paper, 9½ by 12½ inches in size, which is available from Associated Music-Copy Service Corporation (231 West 54th Street, New York, NY 10019). For the out-of-book projects I also suggest that you use a fountain pen that is suitable for writing music; Sheaffer makes an excellent and inexpensive calligraphy model with three point styles. The fine point is best for writing music.

For "Picture Music," (Chapter 14) you will need art paper (the size can vary from 15 by 18 inches to 18 by 20 inches) and several different colored felt-tip markers with large, but not *too* large, tips. Marko by Flair is good.

Bear in mind that neat and legible music expresses clear thinking to your players and leads to a higher level of performance, even in the classroom.

Once You Have Finished This Book

Although several other fine books on composition are currently available, their content is largely theoretical. *Composing Music*, on the other hand, presents entirely practical information that is easy to absorb because you apply it immediately. The experience you will obtain from this book will make you comfortable with a variety of sources and procedures. You will have developed the ability to use these procedures in your own composing. You will have learned the important principles for setting words to music and the way to use many types of music for ideas. You will have developed a good sense of the relationship of the many different parts of composition to the whole. In addition, you will have a valuable reference book of ideas and a set of outlines (in the form of exercises) that you can continue to refer to for future pieces.

Inevitably you will have discovered something important about your own nature and your own ideas.

Lastly I should say that this book has a point of view that would have been considered conservative a few years ago but might be seen as almost daring these days; music *must* have a breadth of thought and feeling that I call *humanistic*—it must be directed to an audience, and it must always be life supporting.

ACKNOWLEDGMENTS

I must give full credit to the two young men who helped me with this book, Jeffrey Ainis and David Stevenson: Jeffrey for his tenacious belief in clarity and directness and for the book's calligraphy; David for his wide scope of knowledge in music and science, as well as for his compositional acuity. Portions of this book were read by Louis Rosen, Sheldon Patinkin, and Jack Kramer, to whom the three of us are thankful for comments and ideas. The entire manuscript was read by Bill Holman, Fred Karlin, and William Allaudin Mathieu, to whom we also wish to express our thanks. The latter two, especially, contributed copious criticism and suggestions, many of which are closely reflected in the book itself. We thank our editor, Lauren Meltzer, for her hard work. None of the people mentioned can be asked to share responsibility for any errors in the book, but only for whatever success we achieve.

Grateful acknowledgment is given to the following for granting permission to reprint material.

To Vicki Goldberg

General Rules
for the Exercises

1. **Prepare yourself for each exercise.** In order to do your best work, it is important to give yourself fully to the exercises. Try to set the right tone, both mentally and emotionally, and strive for stillness of mind. Thorough concentration is crucial.

2. **Get in touch with your voice and your ear.** Sing as you compose and find the tones through what you sing. Playing the piano (or some other instrument) will, of course, help develop your ear, but your main aim should be to get the music in your ear and voice as well as in your mind and fingers. Learn to sing, tone by tone, what you compose, *while* you are composing it. Then you must be able to sing the completed melody—without pause.

3. **Melodies with no harmony or accompaniment should be started and ended on the first tone of the scale (the tonic) and in the same octave as the first tone.** You may *begin* a melody that is harmonized or accompanied on any tone, provided that you *end* on the tonic, preferably *below* the starting tone. This rule will help you stay in one key and will also give shape to your melodies.

4. **Use 2nds and 3rds freely.** Take care with skips and with augmented and diminished intervals. This rule is an expression of the capabilities of the human voice, from which all melody derives. And do not exceed a total range of a major 10th: in other words, the highest and lowest notes of your melody must not be more than a 10th apart.

5. Write for instruments that are available to you. It is important to be able to hear your music played, and it is exciting to see how written music can be transformed into actual sound. Hearing your music will also curb the normal tendency of the beginning composer to go beyond what is playable and practical.

6. The melodies you compose should be written for string instruments or wind instruments. Most of the melodies in the exercises tend to be simple, and string and wind instruments have the capacity to perform this kind of melody with more expression and emotion than other instruments do. The piano is particularly inappropriate for these melodies because it can easily neutralize them. But it is all right to use guitar or piano for a) **harmonies** or b) **accompaniment.**

7. Always specify the tempo and dynamics (including crescendo and decrescendo); indicate whether the notes are to be played legato (by means of slur-phrase markings) or staccato. This rule will encourage you to make your music ready for performance because these indications are as much a part of the music as the notes themselves. (See Appendix B, "Musical Symbols.")

8. Give titles to all of the exercises that are longer than six measures. A title will help you to express a unified mood or idea, and it will also help the instrumentalist perform what you write as *living* music rather than merely as an exercise. It will also help the listener (for whom all composers should have sympathy and affection) understand your music. Make sure that the title expresses the music and that the music expresses the title. Don't use titles that describe the technique you are using (such as "A Special Chord") or titles that give the date of composition ("Tuesday Morning"). Use titles that tell the performer and the listener something about the nature of the music itself.

9. Write mostly in 4/4 and 3/4 meter and use only the following note values, which I call the Basic Note Values:

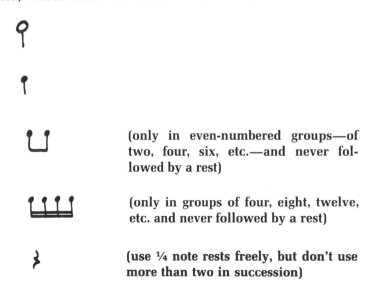

(only in even-numbered groups—of two, four, six, etc.—and never followed by a rest)

(only in groups of four, eight, twelve, etc. and never followed by a rest)

(use ¼ note rests freely, but don't use more than two in succession)

No rests other than the ¼ note rest are allowed. And no ties between notes. As the very last measure of an exercise it is all right to use a note that occupies a full measure—such as a whole note in 4/4 or a dotted ½ note in 3/4.

10. Don't alter the tempo with ritardandos, accelerandos, or fermatas (also called "holds" or "bird's eyes"). These can get in the way of clear rhythmic motion.

The time signatures 3/4 and 4/4, combined with the Basic Note Values, are by far the best rhythmic materials for the developing composer to work with. The above rule will do more to keep you out of trouble and in a direct line with success than any other. You should also restrict the number of different rhythms you use in an exercise; two or three different rhythms will generally serve you better than ten. You may occasionally write in 5/4 or 7/4, if you preserve the division of 5/4 into 2 + 3 or 3 + 2 and the division of 7/4 into 4 + 3 or 3 + 4.

5/4, for example, is often made up of this rhythm (2 + 3):

or this rhythm (3 + 2):

Under no circumstances should you use both of the above rhythms in one melody. In many cases, the division into 2 + 3 (or 3 + 2) is not as easy to see as it is here, but your ear will tell you if you are shifting from one division to another. All of these rules apply to 7/4 also.

Always keep in mind the following: **less is more,** and **silence is music.**

11. Control and restrictions lead to creativity and expansion. From time to time I come across a student who resists the restrictions of this book—especially the General Rules (to which not all of the given examples conform, it should be noted). Such resistance is understandable and you may be feeling it. But let me emphasize the reasons behind these restrictions.

Some restrictions give focus, focus on the procedures at hand—they keep you from having so many choices that you are unable to get in touch with your feelings and ideas. An exercise that asks you to use such-and-such a rhythm and only four given tones is an example of this type of restriction.

Other restrictions are designed to keep you out of trouble. The rule requiring basic note values, for example, helps you to

achieve rhythmic balance, to be able to write a melody that re-
tains its momentum, that keeps going, that does not sag. "Forbid-
den" rhythms, like a measure of dotted 16th and 32nd notes followed by two whole notes, invite trouble for the developing
composer. I want you to be trouble-free when you work with this
book. I want you to be challenged, to feel pleasure and to achieve
excellence.

Finally, these restrictions are a way of not having to pay attention
to anything except what is deep inside of you—**follow the rules
and write the music.**

The Cell, the Row, and Some Scales

1

THE IMPERIAL FLUTE

Imagine that you have been captured by the Lorac, a warlike tribe ruled by Edrevol, who will spare your life only if you please him with the music you write for the Imperial Flute. The Imperial Flute can, however, play only four tones:

Example A

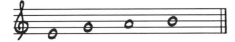

Exercise 1

1. Compose a melody for this four-tone flute, using only the tones shown in Example A.

2. Use only this rhythm (there are no rests in this exercise):

3. To unify your melody and to give it shape, occasionally repeat a measure, either consecutively or after intervening measures.

4. Try not to use all the tones all the time. Study the expressive possibilities of each tone in relation to the other tones. Even though you have four tones to work with, you might consider omitting one tone in the first few measures.

5. Refer to the "General Rules for the Exercises" (p. 1) for the rules that are applicable, here and in all exercises.

The four-note flute is an example of pitch limitation—only four tones or pitches are available for you to use. Pitch limitation will be referred to frequently in this book, as will other forms of limitation of resources. Being subject to limited resources will develop your sense of detail, and it will free you from technical considerations allowing you to concentrate on what you want to express.

THE CELL

The tones of the four-tone flute constitute a limited form of the *cell*, in which you may also use the same tones in other octaves.

Example B

If the cell is made up of the tones shown in *a* of Example B, you may also use the tones shown in *b*, as well as other octave forms of the original four tones.

Here is a melody drawn from Example B. Note that the tone A is used only in the fifth and sixth measures.

Example C

Exercise 2

1. Compose a melody using only the tones of the cell in Example B. You may use octave forms of these tones also.

2. Use only these two rhythms:

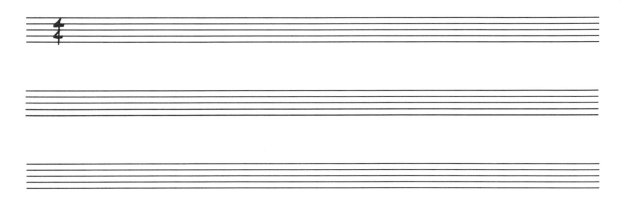

3. Occasionally repeat a measure to help give shape and unity to your melody.

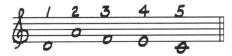

THE ROW

The next pitch-limitation procedure is the *row:*

Example D

In the row, the tones are always used in the same order (1 2 3 4 5, as shown in Example E). In other words, you may not use tone 4 until you have used tone 3; tone 5 must be preceded by tone 4. After using all the tones of the row, start again with tone 1. You may repeat tones (see the repetition of tone 1 in measure 3), but only *immediately* (1 2 2 2 3 4 4 5 1, and so on), and you may use tones in other octaves (see measures 4 and 5).

Example E

Exercise 3

1. Compose a melody that is six to ten measures in length. Use only the row in Example D as well as the octave forms of these tones.

2. Use only these two rhythms:

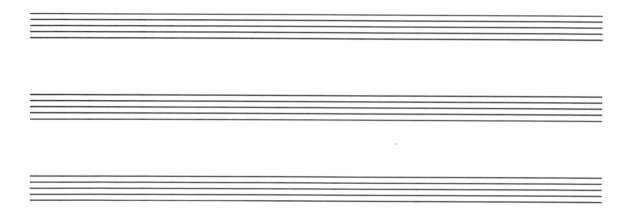

3. Place a number near each of the tones in the melody to show its sequence in the row.

MELODY FROM THE C MAJOR SCALE

This is the C major scale:

Example F

Exercise 4

1. Compose a melody using *only* the tones presented in Example F (and the octave forms of these tones). Consider the melody as a whole, rather than as isolated measures.

2. The first and last tones must be c¹ (middle C).

3. Use only this rhythm:

8

4. Occasionally repeat a measure, either consecutively or after intervening measures. *Hint:* Repeated measures should always be written out in full. Never abbreviate repeated measures because it makes them too easy to use; if you have to write them out completely, you will use them because you really want them.

5. Refer to the General Rules that are applicable, here and in all exercises.

THE DORIAN SCALE

This is the D Dorian Scale:

Example G

It contains the same tones as those in the C major scale, but it centers around the tone D. When you use it for unaccompanied melodies, you must begin and end with the tone D and you must use the tone D frequently; the ear must hear such a melody in the key of D, not C.

Exercise 5

1. Compose a melody of six to ten measures, expressing *water*: a lake, a stream, a waterfall, or rain, for example.

2. Use only the tones in Example G and octave forms of these tones. Don't let your melody slip into C major.

3. Use only this rhythm:

4. From time to time, you may repeat a measure, either consecutively or after intervening measures.

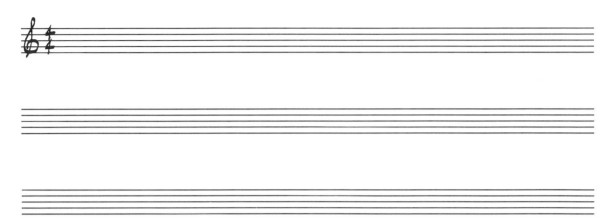

Like the D Dorian scale, the E Phrygian scale shares the tones of the C major scale:

Example H

Exercise 6

1. Compose a melody of six to ten measures. Make it sound dark and ominous.
2. Use only the tones and the octave forms of the tones in Example H. Maintain E as the tonic.
3. Use only these rhythms:

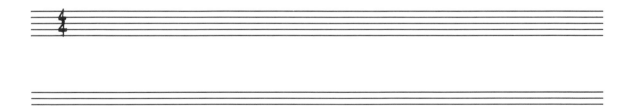

Exercise 7

Write a "mistake exercise" based on Exercise 6. Ignore all instructions and do everything wrong that you can, especially with respect to maintaining E as the tonic. Label all your mistakes.

THE BASIC NOTE VALUES

In all the exercises you have worked on so far, the rhythms have been *given*—that is, you have been restricted to one or two rhythms. This restraint constitutes another limitation of resources, as do the Basic Note Values referred to in the General Rules.

Exercise 8

1. Compose eight to twelve measures for a percussion instrument of indefinite pitch, using only the Basic Note Values. Repeat a measure from time to time. (Note the use of X as a clef sign.)

2. No figurations such as these are permitted:

3. Avoid 8ths or 16ths followed by a rest because such figurations are difficult to perform:

Example I shows six violations of the rules given in Exercise 8.
Try to identify the violations before looking at the Violation List.

Example I

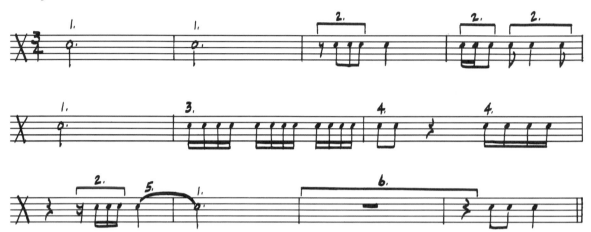

    Violation List
1. Note value not on list of Basic Note Values
2. Figuration not permitted
3. Lack of balance between long notes and short notes
4. Two 8ths or four 16ths followed by a rest
5. Ties not permitted
6. Too many rests

You may feel unduly restricted by the Basic Note Values, but the truth is that hundreds of rhythms can be evolved from them, and many splendid melodies are made up of only two or three rhythms. Restrict yourself to the Basic Note Values and try to work with very few rhythms. Also, make your rhythms fit each other and flow from one into the other.

2

Harmony (I)

**CHORD PROGRESSIONS:
A BEGINNING**

A chord consists of three or more tones sounded simultaneously.
A *triad* is a chord made up of two 3rds. A major triad has a major
3rd on the bottom and a minor 3rd on top; imagine a large box
(a major 3rd) underneath a small box (a minor 3rd). A minor
triad has a minor 3rd on the bottom and a major 3rd on top. The
outer tones of a major or minor triad form a perfect 5th.

Example A

If we construct triads on the tones of the C major scale using
only the tones of this scale, we obtain the following chords,
which are called *diatonic* chords.

Example B

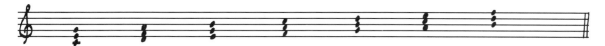

The triads built on C, F, and G are major triads—a major 3rd on
the bottom and a minor 3rd on top. The triads built on D, E, and
A are minor triads—a minor 3rd on the bottom and a major 3rd
on top. The triad built on B is a diminished triad: it is made up
of two minor 3rd's.

13

In popular music, an alphabetical letter by itself indicates a major triad (note that the letter is always capitalized).

Example C

Similarly an alphabetical letter followed by "Min," "Mi," "min," "mi," "m," or a dash (—) indicates a minor triad (I prefer "min").

Example D

A diminished triad is indicated by the alphabetical letter followed by a small zero.

Example E

The seven triads of C major can be represented by alphabetical symbols as shown in Example F.

Example F

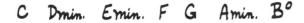

Exercise 1

Write out the tones indicated by these chord symbols:

Now let us discuss chord progression, beginning with the movement of one chord to another. The diminished triad has been excluded from most of this book because it has implications beyond the more fundamental work we are concerned with here.

14

Major or minor triads derived from C major move freely among themselves. Movement between those chords built on the tones that are a perfect 4th or perfect 5th apart is strongest and most propulsive (see Example G, *a*). Next in strength is movement between chords built a 2nd apart (see Example G, *b*). The most neutral movement is between chords built a 3rd apart, especially in diatonic harmony; chords a 3rd apart have two tones in common (see Example G, *c*). Each type of movement is valuable in its own way.

Example G

Exercise 2

Construct various two-chord progressions, using major and minor triads from C major as follows. (Place alphabetical symbols above the staff.)

a) chords a perfect 4th or perfect 5th apart

b) chords a 2nd apart

c) chords a 3rd apart

Hint: Play these progressions over and over. Get to know them.

To construct a *series* of chords, let us begin with these guidelines:

Basic Rules for
Diatonic Chord Progressions

1. Use only diatonic major and minor triads. These may move freely among themselves.

2. The first and last chord must be the triad built on the first step of the scale, the tonic.

3. The root of the next-to-the-last chord must move to the root of the last chord by an interval of a 2nd, 4th, or 5th from above or below.

4. Make sure that the roots of the chords (the tones on which each of the chords is built) form a singable line.

5. Construct your progression so that it points strongly "back home" to the tonic.

Exercise 3

1. Construct a chord progression of eight to ten measures in C major, one chord per measure.

2. Use only major and minor triads derived from the C major scale.

3. Express these chords as alphabetical symbols and give each the duration of a measure.

4. Apply the Basic Rules for Diatonic Chord Progressions.

Example H shows the D Dorian scale followed by the diatonic triads built on each step. These triads are identical with those of C major because D Dorian and C major share the same tones.

Example H

Exercise 4

1. Construct a chord progression of eight to ten measures in D Dorian, one chord per measure.

2. Use only major and minor triads from D Dorian.

3. Write the chords as alphabetical symbols.

4. Apply the Basic Rules for Diatonic Chord Progressions and be especially careful to maintain and support D as the tonic; use the D minor and A minor chords frequently; don't let the progression slip into C major.

Here is the E Phrygian scale, followed by triads built on each of its steps. The chords here are identical with those of C major and D Dorian.

Example I

Exercise 5

1. Compose a chord progression of eight to twelve measures in E Phrygian, one chord per measure.
2. Use only the major and minor triads (no diminished triads).
3. Use alphabetical symbols for this exercise.
4. Apply the Basic Rules again, and be very careful to stay in the key of E Phrygian by using the E minor and A minor chords frequently.

REDISTRIBUTION

A simple way to read chord symbols at the piano is to play the triad in the treble clef and the root of the chord in the bass clef:

Example J

Exercise 6

1. Write out the tones indicated by the symbols in the treble clef.
2. Place the root of each chord in the bass clef.

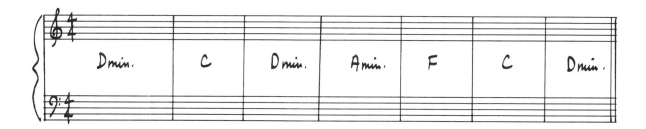

It is easier to play chords in this way if the tones in the right hand (the treble clef) are closer together than in the preceding example. In Example K, I have redistributed the tones of some chords (marked with an asterisk) in order to keep the right hand within as small an area as possible. The root of the chord is still in the left hand.

Example K

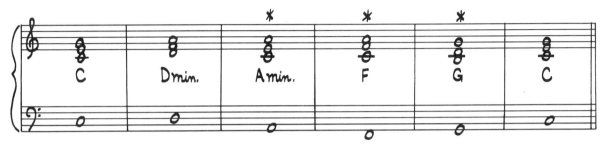

Exercise 7

1. In the treble clef, write out the tones indicated by the symbols, applying the system of redistribution shown in Example K. (In 4/4, two chords per measure indicate that each is a ½ note.)

2. Write out the root of the chord in the bass clef.

3. Play these chords at the keyboard. Redistribution is sometimes weak; be sure it *sounds* right.

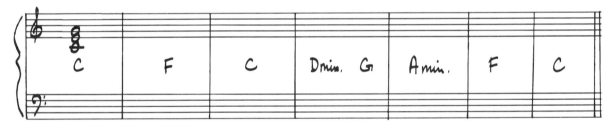

NONDIATONIC CHORD PROGRESSIONS

Until now our chord progressions have been diatonic—drawn solely from the tones in the C major scale. The progression in Example L begins and ends with a C major triad, and it establishes this chord as the tonic, but it contains several chords that are nondiatonic. Note that all the chords are major triads. Play the chords and then play the roots alone.

Example L

18

Example M consists entirely of minor triads:

Example M

Exercise 8

1. In the space given, construct a series of major triads, not restricted to C diatonic chords. Write one chord per measure for as many as fourteen measures. Use symbols only.

2. Begin and end with the same triad. This is *home*, your tonic chord.

3. The root of the next-to-the-last chord should move to the root of the last chord by a major or minor 2nd or a perfect 4th or a perfect 5th, these being the forms of root movement that are most conclusive for a progression.

4. The roots of the chords should form a singable line, and the tonic must be maintained. Be careful with successive chords built on tones an augmented 4th or diminished 5th apart—such root movement is unstable, nervous. Use your ear.

Exercise 9

Construct a series of triads as in Exercise 8, but use minor triads only.

Examples L and M demonstrate a simple rule: Chords of the same type move freely among themselves (a major triad goes freely to any other major triad; a minor triad goes freely to any other minor triad).

When we combine this simple rule with the Basic Rules for Diatonic Chord Progressions, a new set of rules is created that covers a lot of ground. These rules will protect you from some of the basic mistakes that students usually make and they will still allow you to be imaginative and creative.

Basic Rules for Mixed Progressions
1. Use only major and minor triads.
2. Begin and end with a tonic triad (for our purposes, this will be C, D minor, or E minor, from C major, D Dorian, or E Phrygian, respectively).
3. Diatonic triads from within the key may move freely among themselves.
4. A chord of one type may move freely to any other chord of the same type—that is, a major triad, whether it is a diatonic or nondiatonic triad, may move to any other major triad, diatonic or nondiatonic.
5. The root of the next-to-the-last chord must move by 2nd, perfect 4th, or perfect 5th (from above or below) to the root of the last chord.
6. The roots of the chords must support the tonic, and they must form a singable line.

Hint: Fast tempos require simpler progressions and fewer chords than slow tempos.

Example O illustrates the Basic Rules for Mixed Progressions:

Example O

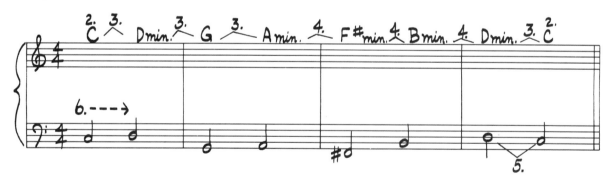

Exercise 10

1. Construct a progression of twelve to sixteen chords according to the Basic Rules for Mixed Progression.
2. Place all three tones of the chord in the treble clef and redistribute them so they move smoothly.

3. Place the root of the chord in the bass clef.

4. Each chord may have the value of a whole note or ½ note.

5. Note the tempo.

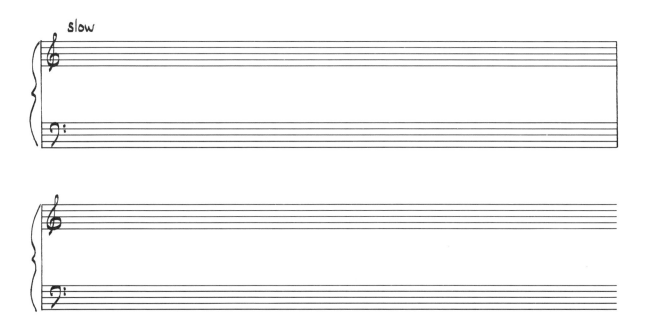

Exercise 11

In the following chord progression there are five violations of the Basic Rules for Mixed Progressions. Find, mark, and label each mistake. Indicate which rule is violated with the appropriate number given on p. 20.

MELODY AND HARMONY

To harmonize a melody, you must find chords that contain the melody tones and that also follow one of the two sets of rules thus far given. For now, let us use the expanded rules—the Basic Rules for Mixed Progressions.

The C major chord in measure 1 in Example P may be followed by either a diatonic triad or a nondiatonic major triad. The tone F in measure 2 is a chord member of two diatonic triads, D minor and F major, and of two nondiatonic major triads, D♭ B♭.

Let us say that you choose to use a B♭ major triad for measure 2 of Example P. This decision means that in measure 3 of Example Q you must go to a major triad—one that contains the melody tone G:

Example Q

Exercise 12

1. Harmonize the following melody according to the process in Example Q, using the Basic Rules for Mixed Progression.

2. Use only one chord per measure, and place the alphabetical symbol above the melody tone.

The next task is to harmonize two tones per chord, both of which must be members of the same chord. In measure 2 of Example R, the D minor triad is diatonic to E Phrygian and may progress to any minor chord or to any diatonic chord that contains the two melody tones. This gives you the choice of two chords, either C or E minor.

Example R

Exercise 13

1. Harmonize the following melody, using the Basic Rules for Mixed Progressions.

2. Use one chord per measure, and place the alphabetical chord symbol above the first ½ note.

3. Strive for balance between the diatonic and nondiatonic chords; too many diatonic chords may make the nondiatonic chords seem inappropriate, and vice versa.

Exercise 14

1. Compose a melody based on the given chord progression.

2. Use only tones that are members of the chord: in measure 2, for example, you may use only B♭, D♭, or F (in any octave).

3. Refer to the General Rules that are applicable, here and in all exercises.

NON-CHORD TONES

Exercise 15

1. Compose a melody to the chords given.

2. You may use tones that are either members of the chord (chord tones) or *passing tones.*

3. A *passing tone* moves by major or minor 2nd between two chord tones a 3rd apart. (Se and Sf are not passing-tone formations because they move by augmented 2nd, which is like a minor 3rd):

Example S

4. A passing tone must not have a greater duration than a ¼ note. Label passing tones "p.t."

5. Use only ¼ notes and ½ notes.

6. The accompaniment may be played by the piano according
to the process shown in Example K.

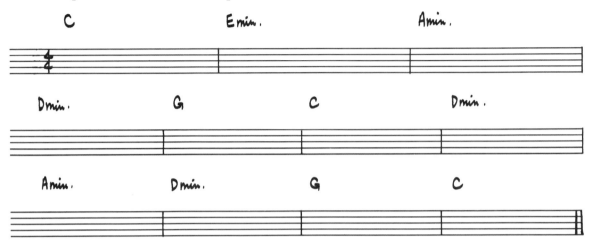

Exercise 16

Compose a melody, as in Exercise 15, but instead of passing
tones, use *neighboring tones*. A *neighboring tone* is a non-chord
tone built a major or minor 2nd above or below a chord tone,
and it is preceded by a skip or a rest. All of the following formations are good:

Example T

Exercise 17

Compose a melody, as in Exercise 15, but instead of passing
tones or neighboring tones, use *auxiliary tones*. An *auxiliary*

tone is a non-chord tone that moves from a chord tone by major or minor 2nd and then returns to the same chord tone:

Example U

Another non-chord tone is the *anticipation tone*, shown in Example V. The anticipation tone always belongs to the chord that follows it, and it is always repeated (*) at the beginning of the following chord.

Example V

Exercise 18

Compose a melody, as in Exercise 15, but use only chord tones and anticipation tones.

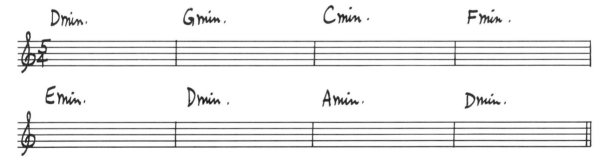

Exercise 19

1. Harmonize the following melody in two ways: Place one set of chord symbols above the staff and a second set below the

staff; if you write further harmonizations, place them on a separate sheet of paper or use a different color pencil.

2. Use the Basic Rules for Mixed Progressions.

3. Employ only one or two chords per measure; try to balance the *rate* of chord-progression movement—use your ear for this.

4. Every tone in the melody must be a chord member of the chord you choose to harmonize it with, except those tones marked with a cross, which are non-chord tones.

5. Each harmonization of the melody will make it sound different and should be given a different title.

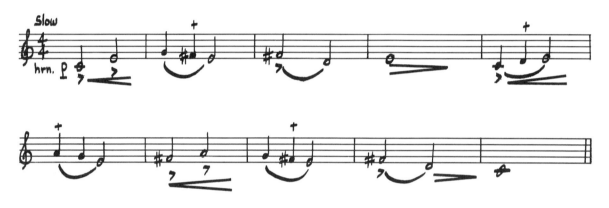

Transformation

MELODIC TRANSFORMATION

Transformation is the process of changing something—of making it different. The first type of transformation is *melodic transformation.* Suppose you have composed this passage:

Example A

It is quite acceptable, but look at it now with one tone, B, flatted:

Example B

This kind of transformation, the adding or subtracting of accidentals, is called *inflection.* Sometimes, as in Example B, you inflect in order to find something different or better; sometimes you inflect in order to make a melody fit the harmony, as in the following exercise.

Exercise 1

1. Example A is written out below. Apply inflection to make it fit the given chords. (The G in measure 3 is a passing tone and need not be a member of the chord.)

    Hint: It is better not to mix sharps and flats as you inflect. This is not a rule, just a caution.

2. Refer to the General Rules that are applicable, here and in all exercises.

Exercise 2

Transpose Example A up a major 2nd. This form of melodic transformation is called *exact transposition*.

If Exercise 2 is correct, you will have an F♯ in the first measure and a C♯ in the second. If you were to change the C♯ to a C♮, you would be inflecting Exercise 2 in exactly the same way that Example B is an inflection of Example A.

Exercise 3

Inflect one or two of the tones in Exercise 2. This change will give you an *inexact transposition* of Example A.

Hint: In general, be consistent with inflection: the tone A occurs here three times; if you inflect it once, you probably should inflect it the same way the other two times.

Example C begins with a repeat of Example A and is followed by an inexact transposition. This example demonstrates another reason for transformation; *it gives you material to carry on with.* (Tones that are inexactly transposed are marked with an asterisk*.)

Example C

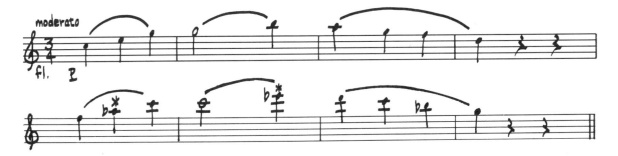

RETROGRADE

Retrograde is another form of transformation. In Example D, you see Example A from back to front; all the tones and rhythms are the same but are reversed.

Example D

Exercise 4

Apply the process of retrograde to measures 1 and 2, following. (Measure 3 will be measure 2 backward, and measure 4 will be measure 1 backward.)

In Exercise 4 you have constructed a *palindrome,* which is a melodic phrase that reads the same backward and forward. In language, familiar palindromes are "Madam, I'm Adam" and "A man, a plan, a canal, Panama." Palindromes are good examples of how transformation can be used to obtain new material.

Always remember that the retrograde may not be interesting to you or that you might like the retrograde better than the original and thus not use the original series of tones at all.

INVERSION

Inversion is another transformational form. *Exact* inversion consists of exactly mirroring the original; a major 3rd up in the original requires a major 3rd down in the inversion, and so forth. In Example E, the lower staff is an exact inversion of the upper. The two are not meant to be played simultaneously.

Example E

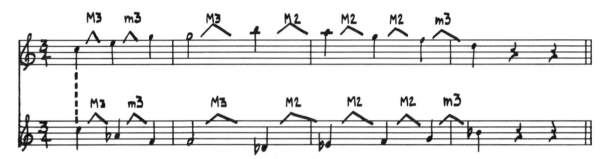

Drawn as a picture, the original and the inversion would look like this:

Example F

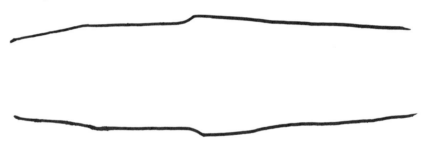

Exercise 5

Write out an exact inversion of the upper tones. Follow the intervals precisely. (If the original ends on the same tone it starts on, so will the inversion.)

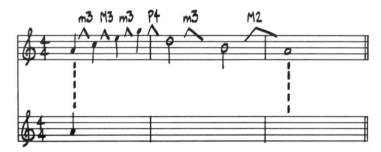

Inexact inversion of the figure is shown in Example G. (The *numbers* of the intervals are the same in the inexact inversion, but a *major* 3rd in the original is *sometimes* answered by a *minor* 3rd in the inversion, and vice versa.)

Hint: Inexact inversion is often used to keep you in the same key.

Example G

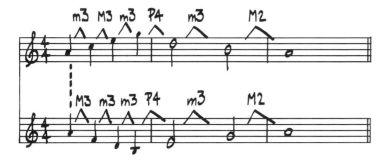

Exercise 6

Write out an inexact inversion of the upper tones. Label each of the intervals in the inversion.

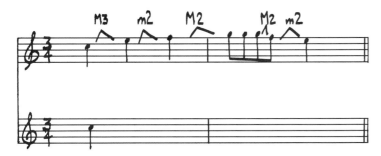

To build up your technique, construct the original and the inversion at the same time—and make them both good (see Example H). Doing this will give you a usable inversion, and you may be able to use it later in a piece. (The original and the inversion do not have to sound good together, but it is easier to construct them both on the *same* staff.)

Example H

Exercise 7

1. Construct an original and an exact inversion at the same time. (They don't have to sound good together, but each has to sound good alone.)
2. Use only tones of D Dorian (the same tones as the C major scale, but starting and ending on the tone D).

3. Follow the given rhythms.
4. Refer to the General Rules that are applicable, here and in all exercises.

RHYTHMIC TRANSFORMATION

The following transformational procedures are rhythmic. The first is displacement, in which a phrase in 4/4 is used, such as:

Example I

In Example J, the phrase is changed to 3/4 (note the accompaniments, which can be clapped if no tambourine is available):

Example J

or kept in 4/4 but started a beat later:

Example K

or changed to 3/4 and started on another beat:

Example L

or started a halfbeat late. In 4/4, this makes all downbeat ¼ notes into upbeat formations (see below) that are not otherwise permitted in these exercises:

Example M

Hint: Displacement works best with some sort of accompaniment. Without accompaniment, the effect of this procedure is usually not clear.

Exercise 8

Here is the given figure:

Change the given figure to 3/4:

Begin the given figure a beat later, in 4/4:

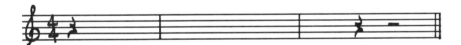

Place the given figure in 3/4 and also start a beat later:

Begin the given figure an ⅛ note later, in 4/4:

Augmentation is another rhythmic transformational procedure. The value of each of the notes in part *b* is twice that of each of the notes in part *a*.

Exercise 9

Apply augmentation to *a*.

Another rhythmic transformation is *diminution*; in Example O, *b*, each of the notes is *half* the value of the original in Example O, *a*.

Example O

Exercise 10

Apply diminution to *a*.

You don't always have to increase the value of the notes by the same proportion. Sometimes you can increase the value of some notes and not others, or decrease some and not others, or increase and decrease in the same phrase, and so forth. Example P is based on Example A. It shows *irregular augmentation* and *irregular diminution*.

Example P

Exercise 11

Use the tones of Example A and apply irregular augmentation and diminution to them.

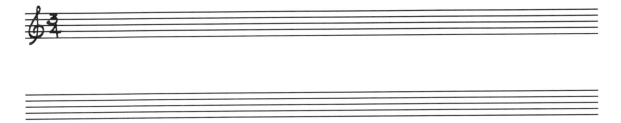

With a very *strong and identifiable* rhythm, as seen in Example Q, you can achieve unity between figurations that have little in common except for this rhythm (see Chapter 6).

Example Q

Exercise 12

Use the rhythm in Example Q and carry it on for four to six measures, using only the tones of the C major scale.

In Example R, some of the tones of Example B have been repeated. This is called reiteration:

Example R

Exercise 13

Apply reiteration to the following melody by making some pairs of ¼ notes into ⅛ notes:

ADDITION AND SUBTRACTION

The next transformational procedure consists of *addition* and *subtraction*, as shown in Example S, in which tones are added to the figuration of Example A.

Example S

In this example, tones are added before and after the original series of tones. In Example T tones are added *internally*—between the tones of Example A. (Non-chord tones are designated with crosses.)

Example T

Exercise 14

Add chord tones and non-chord tones (passing tones, neighboring tones, and auxiliary tones) between the tones of Example A, as shown in Example T. Designate the non-chord tones with crosses. Use your ear.

In Example U, tones from Example A have been subtracted; they have been replaced by rests in *a*; and in *b* the previous tones are held through.

Example U

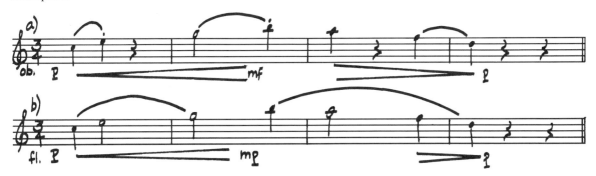

Another form of addition is the use of ornaments, such as trills and grace notes. This kind of ornamentation is prevalent in a great deal of the improvised soul music of today.

Example V

Exercise 15

Add one type of ornament to the melody given.

CONTEXT

The last form of transformation is that of *context*. Play the music in Example W using the chords *above* the staff first. Then play it with the chords *below* the staff. Note the considerable difference between the two versions: *The melody is the same, but it sounds different. This is a change of context.*

Example W

Exercise 16

Evolve new chords for this same melody. The tones marked with a cross may be treated as non-chord tones, but do not use non-chord tones consecutively.

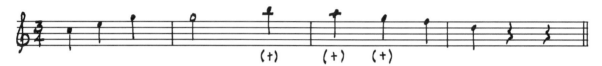

You also change the context by different orchestration and by different tempo, dynamics, expression marks, and articulation (legato or staccato).

Exercise 17

Apply a new set of dynamic and expression marks to part *b*. The melodies in parts *a* and *b* are identical, but you should hear a marked contrast between them.

SUBFIGURATIONS

A series of tones often reveals subfigurations, as seen in Example X, in which six subfigurations are demonstrated:

Example X

Example Y is developed out of subfigurations from Example X.
Note the transpositions:

Example Y

Exercise 18

1. Label at least four subfigurations in the following passage.

2. Write a melody of about eight measures, drawing on the subfigurations you have labeled. You need not use all of them (see Example Y).

3. Use only the tones of D Dorian.

4. Label the subfigurations in the finished melody.

Finding subfigurations and then working with them is an especially rewarding procedure. You will see its compositional relevance in Chapter 4, which deals with the small theme, as well as in later chapters.

APPLICATIONS OF TRANSFORMATION

Transformation is a valuable technique that has several purposes. As suggested earlier, by using the transformational process you will be able to work with and improve your original inspiration.

Secondly, by using it you can alter your initial idea so that it will fit in better with your larger plans. Transformation will also create new material by stretching out an idea. Finally, it will allow you to achieve unity and integrity in your work. If the first theme of your work is outstanding and it also sounds good when inflected, by using the inflected theme later you are adding variety to your piece. These two concepts of unity and variety, which you have heard countless times, will now perhaps assume a clearer meaning.

Theme and variations are a good place to apply transformational procedure, as you will see in the following exercise.

Exercise 19

Be sure to study the General Rules on pages 1 to 3. The theme:

Variation 1: Inflect the original theme in a pleasing manner.

Variation 2: Apply reiteration to the original theme.

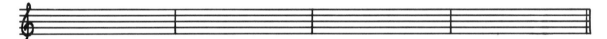

Variation 3: Apply irregular augmentation and diminution, using the tones of the original theme. (You may need more than four measures.)

Variation 4: Write the retrograde of the original theme.

Variation 5: a) The chords express the theme's implied harmony; add tones to the theme, as in Example S,
based on this implied harmony;
    b) Use chord tones, passing tones, neighboring
tones, auxiliary tones, and anticipation tones.
(Label non-chord tones as in Chapter 2.)

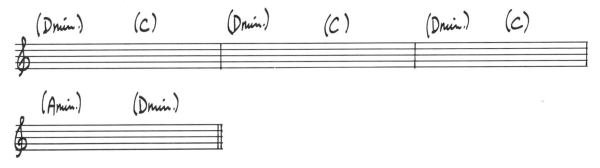

Variation 6: Apply inexact transposition and irregular augmentation to the theme.

Return to the theme.

The Small Theme
and the Large Theme

**THE MOTIVE
AND THE SMALL THEME**

The *small theme* starts with the *motive*, which is a series of tones distinct in shape and yet incomplete; it is usually one or two measures long.

Example A shows a small theme made up of one motive, *a*, repeated exactly and also repeated in transposed form. Note that the transpositions are *tonal*—that is, they correspond to the scale of D Dorian—and that some are exact transpositions and some are inexact. Transpositions of a motive are called *sequences*. In Example A both exact repetitions of the motive and sequences are labeled *a*.

Example A

Exercise 1

1. Compose eight to ten measures in D Dorian based on the motive in the first measure.

2. Repeat the motive, or

3. Repeat the motive in transposed form (exactly or inexactly, according to the tones of the D Dorian scale).

4. Bring the passage to a close with one or two *free* measures in which the motive does not appear.

5. Refer to the General Rules that are applicable, here and in all exercises.

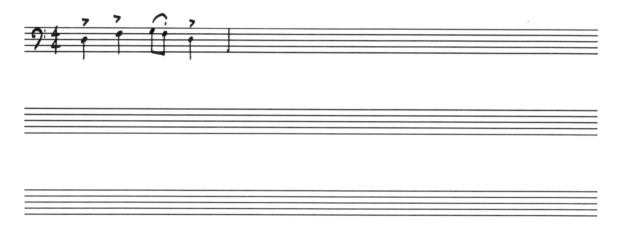

The small theme usually has two, three, or four motives.

Exercise 2

Label the motives in the following passage, as in Example A. Use *a*, *b*, *c*, and so on.

A particularly rewarding arrangement of motives is *a b a c*, in which *a* and *b* pose the question, and *a* and *c* answer it. Play the music in this example and you will understand "question and answer":

Example B

Exercise 3

1. Compose a small theme of four measures based on *a b a c*, as shown in Example B.
2. Use only tones from D Dorian.

Exercise 4

1. Compose a small theme of eight measures for a percussion instrument of indeterminate pitch (tambourine or woodblock are good) or for handclapping if no instrument is available.
2. The theme should be based on *a b a c*, each of which should be two measures long.
3. Make the rhythms compatible with and yet distinct from each other.

MORE ON THE SMALL THEME

Many arrangements of motives are possible in the small theme. A particularly demanding arrangement is *a a b a*, shown in Example C, in which the *a* has three different functions: in measure 1 it constitutes the opening, the beginning; in measure 2 it is a continuation and must lead to *b*; in measure 4 it closes off or concludes the theme. This is a good example of *context*: one motive has three different functions and is heard or perceived in three different ways.

Example C

Exercise 5

Compose a small theme of four measures based on *a a b a*, as in Example C, using tones of the D Dorian scale only.

Sometimes *b* is derived from *a*, as in the following example, where *a* and *b* have the same rhythm (see Chapter 3, Example Q):

Example D

Exercise 6

Write an *a* and a *b* in which each has the same rhythm. Make the rhythm *distinctive*.

If Example D were to be played in a jazz manner, it would sound like this:

Feel free to use this jazz manner in any exercise in the book. Indicate it at the beginning of a piece by writing "uneven 8ths," "a triplet feeling," or "inégales." (*Inégales* is a French word meaning "unequal.") Or you may simply write:

THE LARGE THEME

The small theme in Example E is made up of *a b a c*. Note that it ends on a tone other than the tonic, which makes it unclosed and incomplete:

Example E

Example E constitutes a small theme. Label it with the capital letter A. Now repeat it, changing the last tone to the tonic, C:

Example F

Now play Examples E and F in succession; this will constitute AA, a large theme.

Exercise 7

1. Compose an AA, as seen in Examples E and F.
2. Use only tones in the C major scale and be sure to end the second A on the tone C.
3. Refer to the General Rules that are applicable, here and in all exercises.

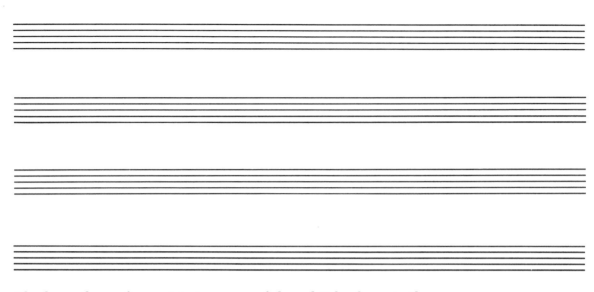

The large theme form, AA, is very useful, and it leads us to the fundamental, *numero-uno*, large-theme form—ABA. An ABA form is made up of one small theme, followed by another small theme, and a return to the first small theme (perhaps altered toward the end):

Example G

THE LARGE THEME, HARMONIZED

These two large-theme forms, the AA and the ABA, are basic to composition, as is the AABA, which is used very frequently in popular music.

The large-theme form can be viewed from the *harmonic* as well as from the melodic standpoint, using the AABA form and restricting ourselves to the tones of the C major scale, melodically and harmonically (except for the B diminished triad, which will not be used here or elsewhere). The following guidelines will be useful:

Guidelines for Harmonization
of the Large Theme

1. Begin each A section with a C chord—the tonic.
2. End the first A section with a C chord, or with D minor, F, or G—the three chords that push back to the tonic.
3. Begin the B section with any of the six available chords, but end it with one of the "pushing chords" (D minor, F, or G).
4. If the B section begins with a C chord, end the second A section with a pushing chord or a C chord.
5. If the B section begins with a chord other than a C chord, you must end the second A section with a C chord.
6. End the last A section with a C chord.

The following example adheres to these guidelines. It is very simple, even more simple than a folk song, but it is a good place to start since it clearly illustrates the relationship between melody, harmony, and form in the construction of a large theme. Note that in this case the motives often begin on the third beat of the measure, whereas until now most motives have begun on the first beat of the measure.

Example H

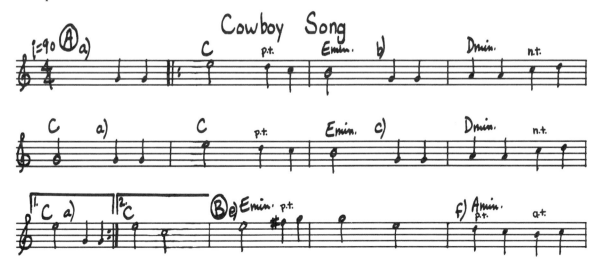

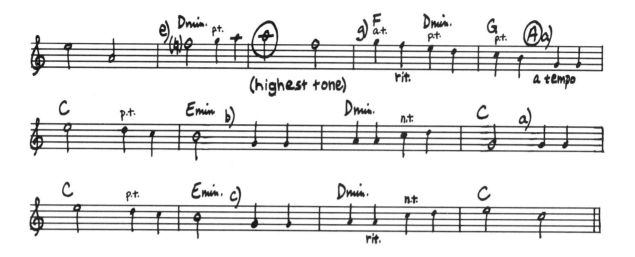

Exercise 8

1. Compose an AABA large theme exactly following the arrangement of motives and small themes given in the following instructions.

2. The three A's are to be made up of *a b a c*.

3. The B section is to be made up of *e e f g*. This gives you a total of six motives in A and B, which is as many as you should use anywhere in this book. You will probably decide to use a sequence (see page 43) for the second *e*, since it is to be built on a different chord from the first *e*.

4. Use chord tones or these non-chord tones: passing tones, neighboring tones, auxiliary tones, and anticipation tones. The non-chord tones must not be longer than a ¼ note, and each must be labeled. Do not use more than one non-chord tone in succession.

5. Try to relate the motives to each other when you can, but also try for contrast in the B section.

6. Your chief aim in B is to make it sail back into the last A section.

7. Let the highest tone occur in B. This will give a natural curve to the entire melody.

The guidelines for the harmonization of the large theme are designed to keep you tightly reined, so that the relationship between melody, harmony, and form can be controlled carefully. But you should feel free, later on, to use nondiatonic chords, as per the Basic Rules for Mixed Progressions.

When you use these rules, Instead of limiting yourself to the "pushing chords" in C major—D minor, F, and G—you may use *any* chord that has a *pushing function*. In other words, you may use any chord derived from the Basic Rules for Mixed Progressions that is built on the tone a major or minor 2nd or a perfect 4th or a perfect 5th above or below the tonic. And you may also use D as the tonic, in D Dorian, and E as the tonic, in E Phrygian.

VISUAL FORMS OF MELODY

Making a graph of a melody is very useful because it reveals something about the *shape* of the melody. In the following graph, I have shown the melody from Example G.

Example I

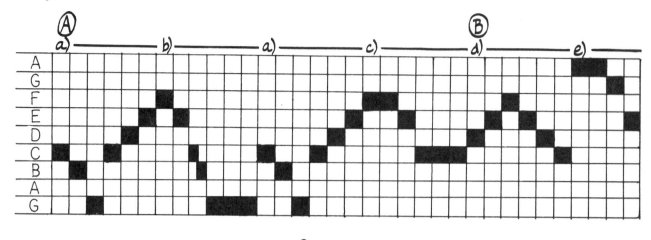

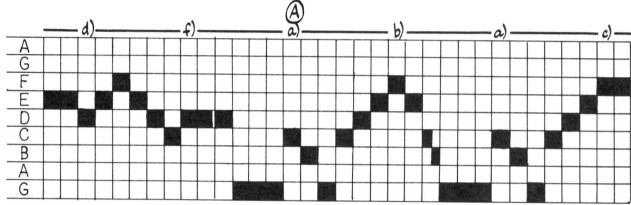

A good melody generally has an upper curve and a lower curve. In other words, its highest tone occurs a little after the midpoint. The upper curve is more important than the lower curve. Both curves occur gradually, and you will note that there are smaller curves within the main curve.

These are general observations about melody; not all melodies fit these observations, but they will guide you in composing a melody, and they will help you to improve your melody when it seems as if something is lacking.

The most important thing about melody writing is that it must come from your voice and from your vocal capabilities. You must be able to *hear* what you write, and you should also be able to sing it. If your ear and voice need improvement, this is the time to begin. There is no better way to help your ear and your voice than to sing what you compose and to compose only what you can sing. There is no better way to help your composing.

Exercise 9

Make a graph of the melody that you composed for Exercise 8. Each space from left to right (horizontally) represents a ¼ note. Each space from top to bottom (vertically) represents a tone of the chromatic scale. The measures are marked out.

a)　　　　b)　　　　a)　　　　c)

| E |
| D♯E♭ |
| D |
| C♯D♭ |
| C |
| B |
| A♯B♭ |
| A |
| G♯A♭ |
| G |
| F♯G♭ |
| F |
| E |
| D♯E♭ |
| D |
| C♯D♭ |
| C |
| B |
| A♯B♭ |
| A |
| G♯A♭ |
| G |
| F♯G♭ |
| F |
| E |
| D♯E♭ |
| D |
| C♯D♭ |
| C |
| B |
| A♯B♭ |
| A |

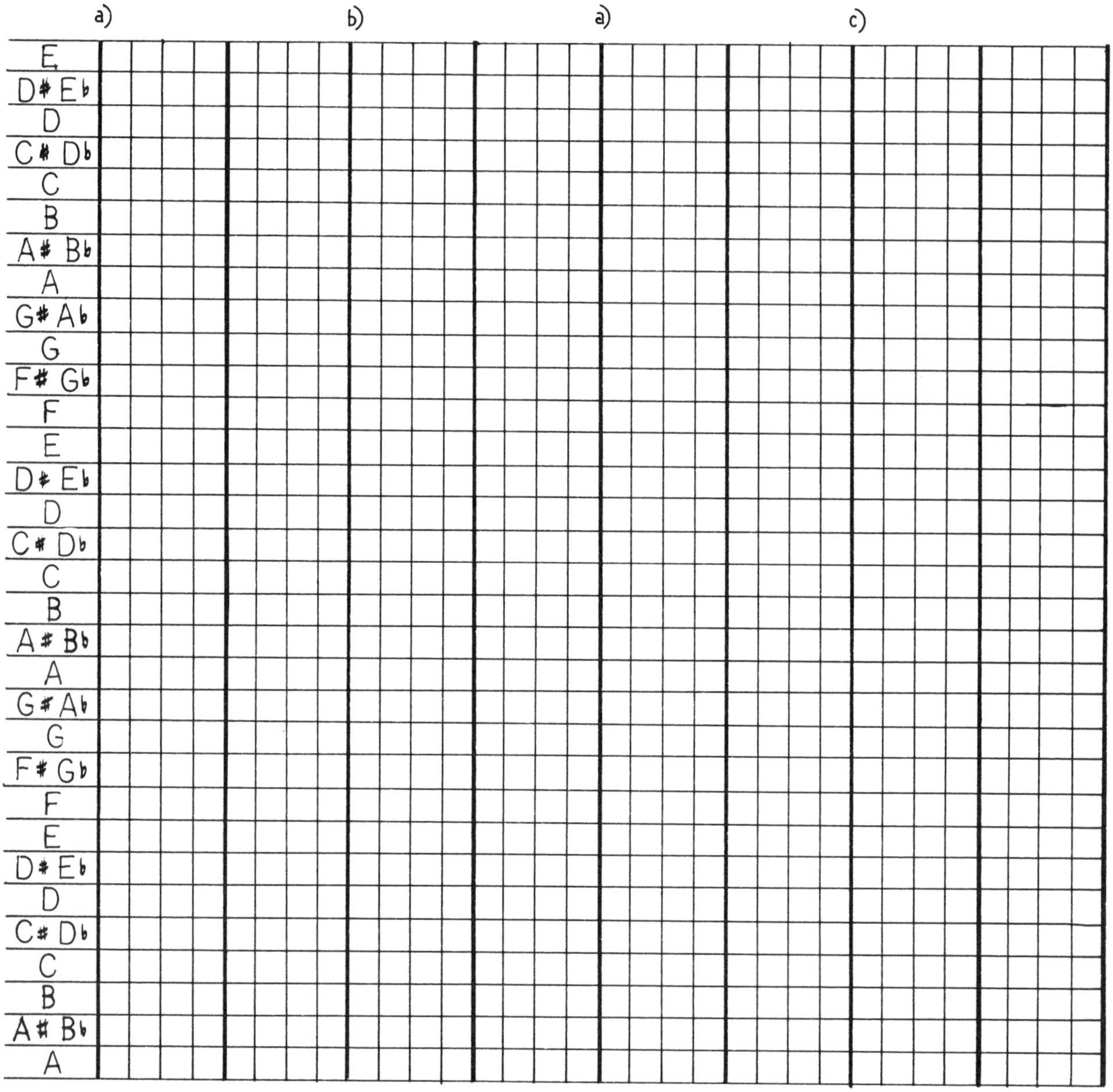
a)
b)
a)
c)
E
D# Eb
D
C# Db
C
B
A# Bb
A
G# Ab
G
F# Gb
F
E
D# Eb
D
C# Db
C
B
A# Bb
A
G# Ab
G
F# Gb
F
E
D# Eb
D
C# Db
C
B
A# Bb
A

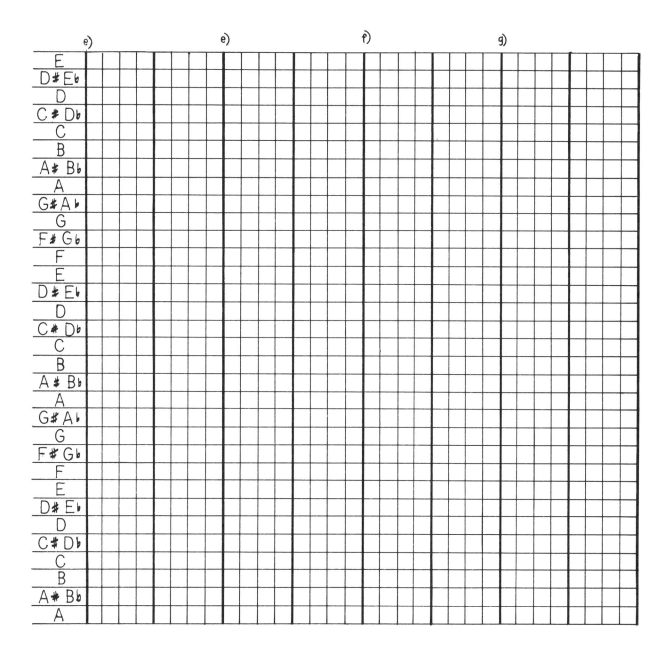

a) b) a) c)

Note
E
D#E♭
D
C#D♭
C
B
A#B♭
A
G#A♭
G
F#G♭
E
E
D#E♭
D
C#D♭
C
B
A#B♭
A
G#A♭
G
F#G♭
F
E
D#E♭
D
C#D♭
C
B
A#B♭
A

More Scales
and the 12-tone Row

THE PENTATONIC SCALE

This is the pentatonic scale, which is made up of five tones. It consists of the black keys on the piano:

Example A

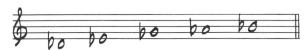

Since this book uses as few flats and sharps as possible, let us raise this scale a minor 2nd by taking away all five flats:

Example B

Just as the C major scale may be arranged in more than one order (D dorian, E Phrygian), so may the pentatonic scale:

Example C

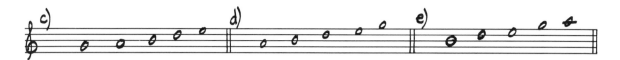

The most "American" form is the E pentatonic scale, as shown in b, Example C.

Exercise 1

1. Compose a small theme eight measures long.
2. Use only the tones of the E pentatonic scale in any octave.
3. Follow the *given* rhythms that are written beneath the staff.
4. Harmonize this theme with chords from E Phrygian, according to the Basic Rules for Diatonic Chord Progressions. You may treat some tones as passing tones, neighboring tones, auxiliary tones, and anticipation tones when they function as such. Remember, all non-chord tones must be a ¼ note's duration or less. Label all non-chord tones. All other tones must be treated as chord tones; they must belong to the triad in question. Use alphabetical symbols.
5. Refer to the General Rules that are applicable, here and in all exercises.

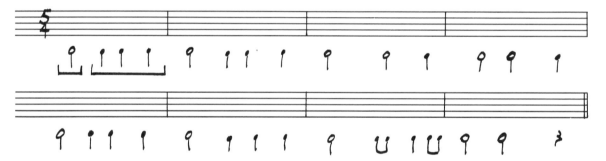

THE DITONIC SCALE

A very interesting scale is the *ditonic* scale, shown in Example D. (It should not be confused with the *diatonic* scale.) Like the pentatonic scales shown in Example C it is also a five-note scale, but it has a much more "major" quality than the other pentatonic scales.

Example D

Exercise 2

1. Compose a small theme—a march—eight to twelve measures long.

58

2. Use only the tones of the C ditonic scale, in any octave.

3. Harmonize this melody with chords from C major, and follow the rules for harmonic treatment in Exercise 1.

4. Construct a one-measure rhythm and use only this rhythm throughout.

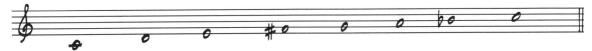

C LIXIAN:
AN INVENTED SCALE

A couple of years ago, I started working with a scale that I call the "Lixian" scale:

Example E

I found this scale very stimulating, as did my students. Here is a passage in which this scale is used. Try to hear it played, or play it on the piano.

Example F

Exercise 3

1. Compose a six-to-ten-measure small theme using only the tones of the C Lixian scale. Be sure to use *all* the tones of this scale, so that you represent it clearly.

2. The notes below the staff may be played by any percussion instrument. Be sure to *line up* these notes with the melody, so that simultaneously sounded notes are directly above and below each other:

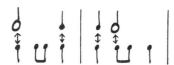

3. Use no more than three different one-measure rhythms.

THE BLUES SCALE

The last scale in our small list of scales is the "blues scale," indicated in Example G. This is the pentatonic scale starting on

E, with the added tone of B♭. Play it and you will recognize it immediately.

Example G

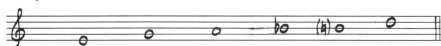

Exercise 4

1. Compose a *work song*, a small theme of eight to twelve measures, preferably for an instrument that is used in jazz or blues, such as the trumpet, trombone, or saxophone.
2. Use only the tones of the blues scale, in any octave.
3. Use only the three rhythms shown in *a*. (The first is the best for the final measure.)

TRANSPOSING THE SCALES

All these scales may be transposed—that is, they may be constructed on tones other than those shown here. The Lixian scale, for example, is made up of seven tones. The second tone is a major 2nd above the first, and so on:

Example H

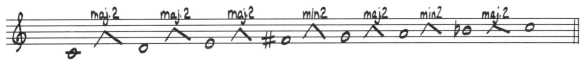

If you want to construct the Lixian scale on the tone F, build it, step by step, in the same relationship you see in Example H.

Example I

Exercise 5

Construct the Lixian scale on these tones:

Exercise 6

Construct the Dorian scale on these tones:

Exercise 7

Construct the Phrygian scale on these tones:

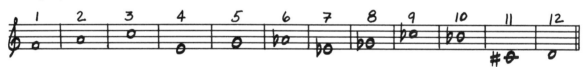

THE 12-TONE ROW

The row was introduced in Chapter 1. The *12-tone row* was formulated by Arnold Schoenberg early in the twentieth century. Example J shows such a row, consisting of all twelve tones found in the chromatic scale.

Example J

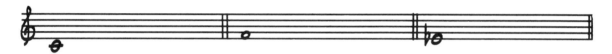

To compose a melody from such a row, you must use the tones only in the original order (1 2 3 4 5 6, and so on). However, you may repeat a tone *consecutively* (1 2 3 3 3 4 5, and so on). You may use tones from the row in any octave. Example K shows a melody based on these simple rules, using the row shown in Example J.

Example K

Exercise 8

1. Compose a melody of eight to sixteen measures using the 12-tone row in Example J.

2. The integrity of such a melody is in the ordering of the tones, so you need not try to achieve a small-theme form here. (It is difficult to achieve small-theme form from the row.)

3. You must use the tones only in the original order, but you may use octave forms of the row and you may repeat tones immediately (as in measure 5 of Example K).

4. Use the row more than once if you wish. Try to end on the tone F, in the same octave as the first tone.

5. Use only this rhythm:

6. End with:

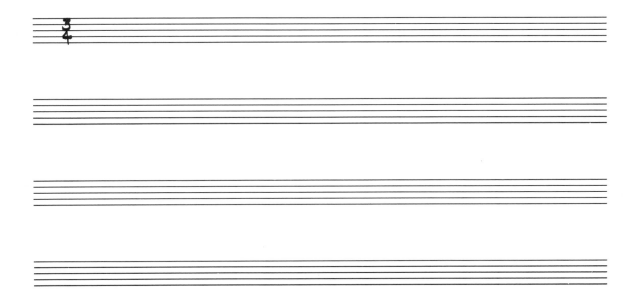

It is characteristic of 12-tone procedures to use not only the original row but also the retrograde, the inversion, and the retrograde of the inversion:

Example L

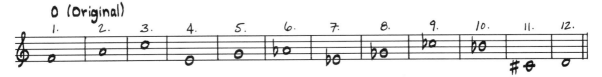

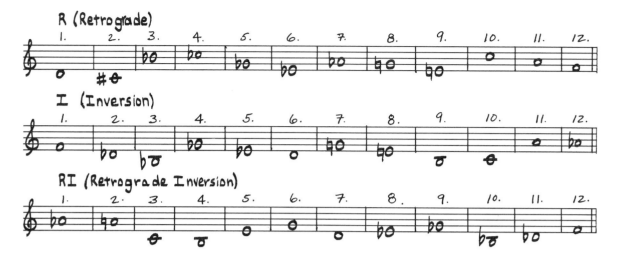

Sometimes these four forms are used consecutively, in a single voice. Sometimes the original is used in one voice, the retrograde in another, and so on. It is also possible to use the row *vertically*—that is, as chords. This subject is discussed indirectly in Chapter 9.

Exercise 9

1. Compose a piece of forty to sixty measures, based on the four forms of the row shown in Example L.

2. Divide the row into four sections, each of approximately the same length. Use a different form of the row in each of the four sections. For example, O I R RI or R RI O R, and so on.

3. Follow the rules that precede Example K.

4. The last form of the row in each section does not need to be complete. Use your ear to guide you toward a home base for the entire piece—toward a tone that rounds off the piece.

5. Stretch your abilities in this exercise. You may use a range of up to two and a half octaves, you may write a less singable melody, and you may use a greater variety of rhythms—all of which are characteristics of 12-tone music. Make sure you are able to hear what you compose and that it sounds right to you.

6. Label the exercise carefully: specify the form of the row that you are using at the beginning of each section and number each tone from 1 to 12.

7. Use separate manuscript paper for this exercise and write your final draft in ink.

Exercise 10

Construct your own 12-tone row, based on the following considerations:

1. It should use all 12 tones of the chromatic scale, without repetition.
2. The notation should be freely enharmonic; use flats, sharps, and naturals and do not use double flats or double sharps.
3. Avoid using one interval too often.

Isomelody and Isorhythm, Combined

ISOMELODY

An *isomelody* is a series of tones that is repeated one or more times. Example A shows a six-tone isomelody:

Example A

Note that tones 1 and 4 are the same, as are tones 3 and 5. Example B shows a melody that is made up of the tones of the isomelody:

Example B

In an isomelody, one tone may be used more than once, as in Example B, but each tone of the isomelody may be used only as originally given (1 2 3 4 5 6 always; never 1 1 2 3 4 4 5 6). You may not use octave forms of the tones in an isomelody. In these two respects, the isomelody is different from the row (Chapter 1) and the 12-tone row (Chapter 5).

Exercise 1

1. Compose a theme that is ten to twenty-six measures long, based on the isomelody given in Example A.
2. Use the tones in the order given (1 2 3 4 5 6). Repetition of tones is not permitted (1 1 2 3 4 4 5 6). You may not use octave forms of the tones.
3. Use ¼ notes and ½ notes only.
4. Number each tone of the melody, as shown in Example B.
5. Refer to the General Rules that are applicable, here and in all exercises.

ISORHYTHM

An *isorhythm* is a rhythm that is repeated consecutively (see Example Q, Chapter 3):

Example C

Exercise 2

Write an isorhythm.

Exercise 3

Compose a melody based on the isorhythm given beneath the staff, using only tones from the C Lixian scale.

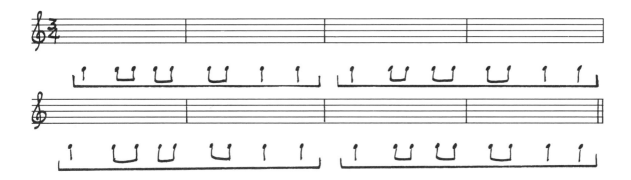

ISOMELODY AND ISORHYTHM COMBINED

If an isomelody of four tones is combined with an isorhythm of four notes exact repetition is achieved; the isomelody and the isorhythm are "in-sync":

Example D

An isomelody and isorhythm that are "in sync," as in Example D, constitute an *ostinato*—a form that will be dealt with separately in Chapter 7.

If the isomelody and isorhythm are "out of sync," they form patterns that first change and then come together:

Example E

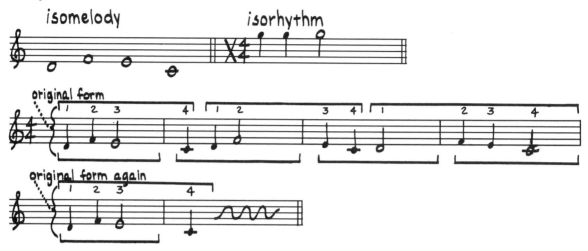

The term "original form" used in Example E serves to designate the relationship between the isomelody and isorhythm as they first appear.

Exercise 4

Write a four-tone isomelody using tones of the E pentatonic scale (E G A B D):

Exercise 5

1. Combine the isomelody in Exercise 4 with this isorhythm:

2. Bracket the isomelody above the staff and the isorhythm below the staff.

3. Keep going until the original form reappears.

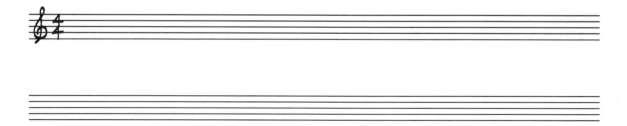

In Exercise 5 the original form of the combined out-of-sync isomelody and isorhythm will come together after twenty beats. When longer isomelodies and isorhythms are combined out of sync, they may require many more beats to come together. In Example F the isomelody is made up of seven tones and the isorhythm is made up of nine notes; the original form reappears in measures 15 and 16. In other words, it takes fifty-six beats, or fourteen measures, for the out-of-sync isomelody and isorhythm to come together again:

Example F

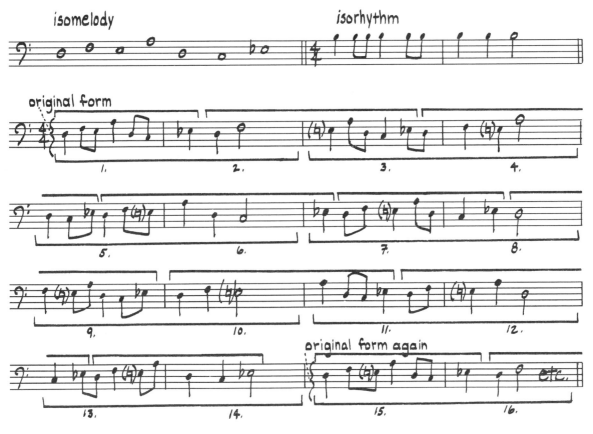

Exercise 6

1. Write an isomelody of eight tones based on the C ditonic scale (C E F G B) and combine it with the given seven-note isorhythm.

2. Mark the isomelody with brackets.

Exercise 7

1. Write an out-of-sync combined isomelody and isorhythm based on the C ditonic scale.

2. Bracket the isomelody above the staff and the isorhythm below the staff.

3. Refer to the General Rules that are applicable, here and in all exercises.

Exercise 8

An effective way to use a combined out-of-sync isomelody and isorhythm is as accompaniment; this use is shown in the bass clef of *b* in this exercise.

1. Compose a melody to this accompaniment, using no rests and only these note values:

72

2. Use chord tones and neighboring tones. The neighboring tones must be ¼ notes and must be labeled.

3. Do not use a neighboring tone in the melody at the same time that a non-chord tone occurs in the accompaniment.

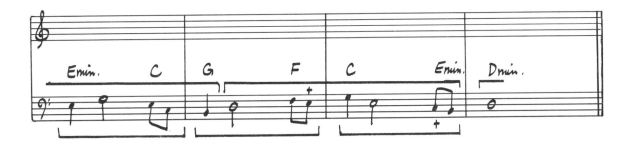

Exercise 9

1. Harmonize the following isomelody and isorhythm in either E Phrygian or C major; employ the Basic Rules for Mixed Progressions.

2. Use one or two chords per measure.

3. Mark tones that you are treating as non-chord tones with a cross.

Ostinato

OSTINATO AS ACCOMPANIMENT

The *ostinato* consists of an isomelody and an isorhythm that are in sync.

Example A

It is usually—but not always—a lower part, and it is often assigned to a bass instrument, such as the tuba, double bass, or bassoon.

Exercise 1

1. Write an ostinato in the bass clef, using only tones of D Dorian, within the range of an octave.
2. Play it or sing it several times in succession, to make sure that it will bear repetition.
3. Refer to the General Rules that are applicable, here and in all exercises.

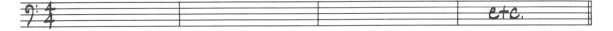

OSTINATO LINKED
TO THE HARMONY

In popular music, the ostinato usually "moves along with the chord"—that is, it will have the same relationship to the second chord that it has to the first chord, and so on.

Example B

Also, in popular music the ostinato is often made up of the root and the 5th of the chord, plus the tone a minor 7th above the root:

Example C

Exercise 2

Write a characteristic pop ostinato like those in Examples B and C based on the given chords. Write for piano. Play the chords with the right hand and the ostinato with the left.

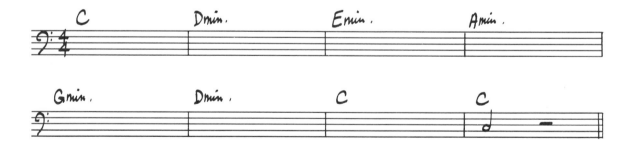

Exercise 3

1. Compose the first three measures of a melody that will fit the following ostinato pattern taken from Example C.

2. Use chord tones only.

3. Use only these note values:

Exercise 4

When you are going to use an ostinato that moves along with the chords, whether pop or not, you can write the ostinato *after* the melody. Write an ostinato for the given melody and chords shown in this exercise. Use basic note values only. Write the ostinato in the bass clef. (The crosses in the next-to-the-last measure designate non-chord tones.)

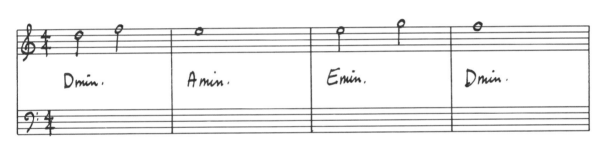

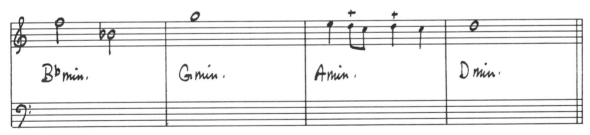

OSTINATO RESISTING
THE HARMONY

Ostinato works well when it *resists* chords, too; the chords change but the ostinato keeps repeating without change. (Incidentally, *ostinato* is the Italian word for "stubborn" or "obstinate".) Notice that the ostinato seems to *sound different* when the chord changes (another example of *context*) and that the tension increases, especially in measures 5 and 6:

Example D

When the ostinato is used this way, there is a point where the harmony and ostinato should come together, either where the harmony returns to the original chord, as in Example D, or where the ostinato finally is transposed to fit the chord, as in Example E.

Example E

Exercise 5

1. Construct a series of chords for the ostinato given. Allow the chords to move away from the tones in the ostinato, as shown in Examples D and E. Be aware of increases and decreases in tension.

2. You should construct these chords according to the Basic Rules for Mixed Progressions (Chapter 2). Use one chord per measure.

OSTINATO WITHOUT CHORDS

A good way to compose melody and ostinato *without* chords is to use a simple cell, such as the one made up of the notes E, A, and B shown in Example F. This kind of cell produces very little friction between melody and ostinato, and your ear alone should be able to guide you. This procedure does not, however, work with all cells for reasons that are explained in Chapters 11 and 12.

Example F

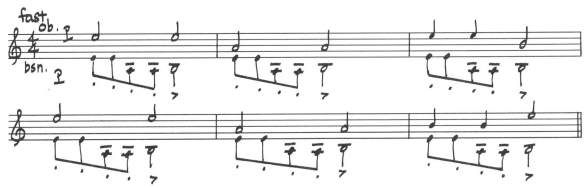

Exercise 6

1. Compose a melody and an ostinato, as in Example F; use the same cell—E A B.

2. Give the melody and the ostinato elbow room—never let one cross above or below the other.

Another way to compose melody and ostinato without chords is to use the pentatonic scale, which, like the cell in Example F, is also relatively "frictionless." Example G uses the tones of the E pentatonic scale (E G A B D):

Example G

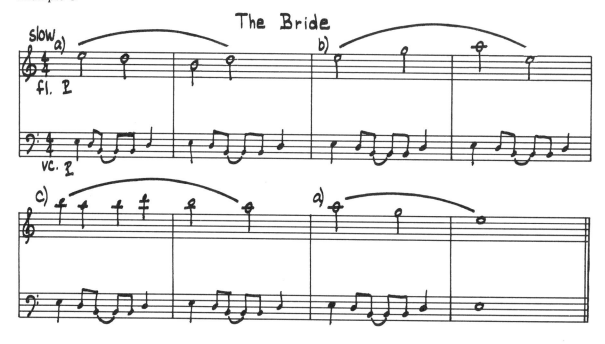

Exercise 7

1. Compose a melody and an ostinato using only the tones of the E pentatonic scale; use Example G as a guide.

2. Refer to the General Rules that are applicable, here and in all exercises.

Exercise 8

The primary use of ostinato is as accompaniment, but it is also useful for introductory or linking passages.

1. In the space given compose an ostinato of four to six measures in the treble clef that will act as an introductory passage leading to the large theme given in Example H (Chapter 4).

2. The chords should be evolved from the Basic Rules for Diatonic Chord Progressions, but you must bear in mind that you should not try for a *closed* chord progression beginning and ending on the tonic, but an *opening* chord progression, leading toward the tonic. In other words, the last chord should be a 2nd, 4th, or 5th above or below C—the root of the first chord of the large theme.

3. Use one chord per measure; allow the ostinato to move along with the chords (pop style) or to resist the chords.

Accompaniment Procedures

FORMS OF THE "OOM-PAH"

A basic accompaniment figuration is the "oom-pah"; it is named after the marching-band style in which the tuba plays the "oom" and the horns the "pah." (This accompaniment is surprisingly simple, but I didn't recognize its usefulness until late in my own career.)

Example A

For now, think of it as a piano part, left hand only, with the "oom" as the root of the chord and the "pah" as the 3rd and the 5th.

Exercise 1

Write an oom-pah accompaniment to the given chords.

Another form of this accompaniment is "oom-pah-pah":

Exercise 2

1. Compose a small theme suggested by and appropriate to the accompaniment given. The form *a b a c* is one possibility.

2. Make sure that this melody is *above* the range of the accompaniment. Both the melody and the accompaniment must have their own space—their own elbow room.

3. Use only chord tones and auxiliary tones (label them "a.t."). No auxiliary tone should be longer than a ¼ note in duration.

4. Assign the melody to an available wind or string instrument and the accompaniment to piano (left hand only).

5. Refer to the General Rules that are applicable, here and in all exercises.

Oom-pah and oom-pah-pah accompaniments also may be played by wind and string instruments:

Example C

and have numerous other forms, some of which are shown here:

84

ARPEGGIC ACCOMPANIMENTS

The following accompaniment procedures are *arpeggic*; that is, in the arpeggio style. They are made up of chord tones, sounded in succession. The most widely known arpeggic form is the *Alberti bass*, named after the 18th Century composer who made it popular:

Example E

Exercise 3

The basic pattern of the Alberti bass is root-5th-3rd-5th, as shown in Example E. Use this pattern to write an Alberti bass for the given chords. Write in the treble clef if you wish; accompaniment procedures need not be limited to the bass clef.

In Example F, the usual Alberti-bass pattern doesn't work well; it is awkward and wandering:

Example F

When the roots of successive chords are farther apart than a 2nd, as they are in Example F, you can achieve smooth movement in the Alberti bass by *redistributing* the tones of the chord (see Chapter 2), so that the first tones of successive chords are the same or a 2nd apart.

Example G

Exercise 4

1. Write an Alberti bass to the given melody, and redistribute as necessary. (The first measure has been written out.)

2. In the last measure, use root-5th-3rd-5th, in order to bring the passage to a close.

Journey

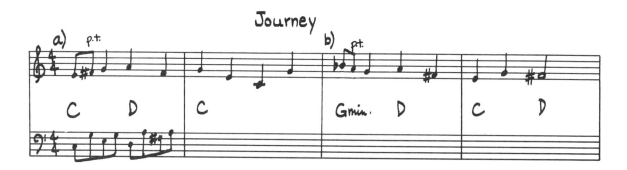

Here are some other arpeggic patterns. Redistributed chords are indicated by an asterisk:

Example H

Exercise 5

1. Write an arpeggic accompaniment drawn from the given chords. Use redistribution here too.

2. Use only the pattern given in the first measure.

Exercise 6

Write an accompaniment, using redistribution, according to the rules in Exercise 5.

Exercise 7

1. Compose a melody to the accompaniment shown.

2. Use the given rhythms to construct this melody.

3. Use only chord tones and passing tones (label these).

4. If possible, use transformational procedures, especially those based on subfigurations (see Chapter 3).

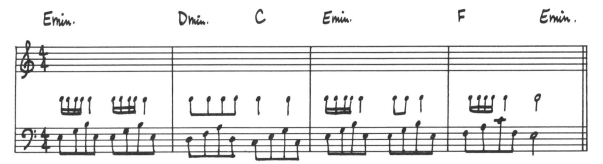

REPEATED-CHORD ACCOMPANIMENTS

Repeated chords are another excellent form of accompaniment (note the redistributions indicated by asterisks):

Example I

Exercise 8

Write a repeated-chord accompaniment to the following chords, as shown in Example I. Write for piano, in the bass clef, left hand only.

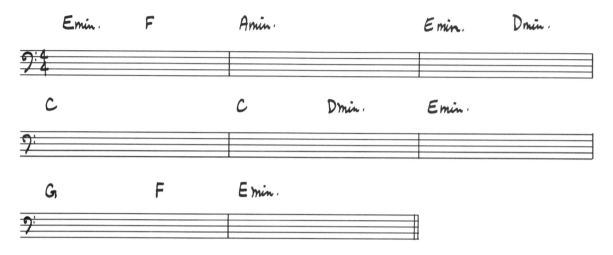

Other forms of repeated chord accompaniment are shown in Example J: *a*) the "silent downbeat" in 4/4 (note that melody is always present on the first beat of the measure); *b*) the silent downbeat in 3/4; *c*) "the Boston," a New Orleans jazz form that is suitable for any kind of music; *d*) "the false waltz," which is like oom-pah-pah with an extra beat; and *e*) "the claw," which is found in both Mozart and Italian rock-and-roll.

Example J

Exercise 9

1. Construct a chord progression in D Dorian for an ABA large-theme form, employing the Basic Rules for Mixed Progres-

sions. Consult the Guidelines for Harmonization of the Large Theme (see Chapter 4).

2. Then compose an accompaniment for this chord progression using one accompaniment for both A's and a contrasting accompaniment for the B. The accompaniment to A and B should be chosen from Example J, above.

3. You will end up with an accompaniment without melody, which should help you to see how accompaniment and harmony contribute to structure and form.

AFTERTHOUGHTS

A very interesting accompaniment procedure is the *reiterated tone*, which is shown in Example K. This kind of pattern may change to fit each of the chords (as in *a*) or resist them (as in *b*); this process was demonstrated in the discussion of ostinato in Chapter 7.

Example K

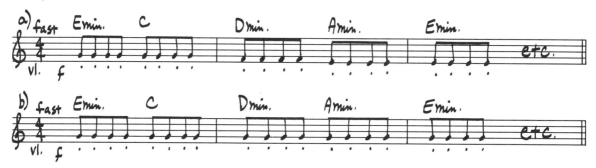

There are two more points I would like to make about accompaniment and harmony. First, sometimes the accompaniment and melody are based on a cell or a scale instead of on a chord (see pp. 79–80 for examples). Second, sometimes the accompaniment is made up of only one chord—a topic dealt with in Chapter 9.

Harmony (II)

THREE SPECIAL CHORDS

Some chords are interesting enough to be considered individually. One such chord is Alexander Scriabin's "mystic chord," which he used to generate entire pieces:

Example A

Exercise 1

1. Compose a melody to the accompaniment given, which is made up exclusively of tones of the mystic chord. Repeat the first measure of the accompaniment as many times as you wish.

2. Use only the tones of this chord for your melody, in any octave. (In other words, this chord is your cell.)

3. Use a small theme form, if you wish. Repeat measures from time to time. Strive for shape.

4. Refer to the General Rules that are applicable, here and in all exercises.

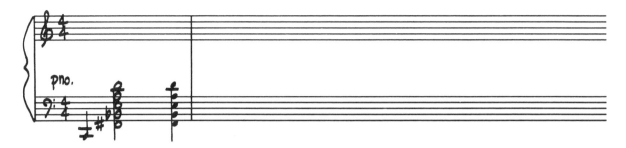

Example B contains a chord called the "Hendrix chord." Jimi Hendrix was fond of it.

Example B

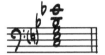

Exercise 2

1. Write two different repeating accompaniment patterns, using only the tones of the Hendrix chord. One of the two should be arpeggic.

2. To make sure that the arpeggic pattern, which is a *horizontal* series of tones, is perceived *vertically* (that is, as a chord), be sure to use *all* the tones of the chord in your accompaniment and to avoid spreading them out over too many beats.

a)

b)

Here is another special chord—one that I have used extensively:

Example C

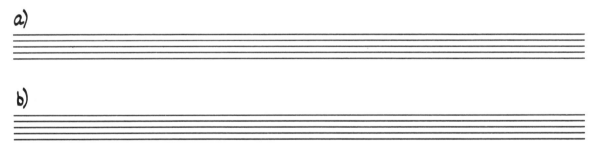

Exercise 3

1. Write an ostinato accompaniment pattern for cello or an available low-string instrument that shows off the chord in Example C; use tones of this chord only. (Use *all* the tones!)

2. Compose a small theme to this accompaniment using tones of the chord only; write it for flute or an available treble-clef instrument.

3. Remember to listen to the chord carefully before you start and to refresh yourself periodically.

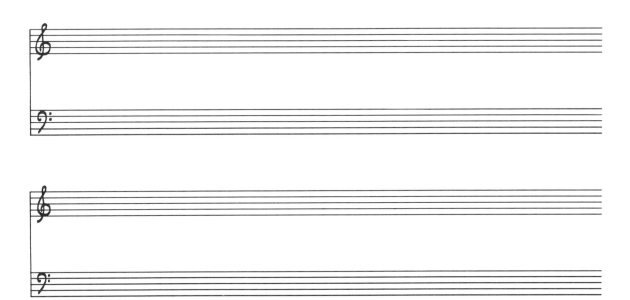

MORE NON-CHORD TONES

The work you have done in the first part of this chapter has been severely restricted to chord tones. Now let us turn to non-chord tones, a topic that was first discussed in Chapter 2.

We have seen how non-chord tones can open up a melody, even within the modest harmonic framework so far developed. A melody made up exclusively of chord tones tends to be solid, but solidity is not always interesting. Non-chord tones add tension and excitement when used carefully; used carelessly they tire the ear.

Changing tones are two tones, neither of which is in the chord, that are built a major or minor 2nd below and above (or above and below) a chord tone, to which they "resolve":

Example D

Exercise 4

1. Compose a small theme based on the harmony given, using only chord tones and changing tones (which must be labeled). The chords are diatonic to D Dorian, but you need not restrict yourself to diatonic changing tones if you use great care.

2. Changing tones should not be longer than ⅛ notes, except in fast tempos.

A *reverse neighboring tone* is preceded by a chord tone a major or minor 2nd above or below it, and it is followed by a *skip* (a movement larger than a major 2nd) to a chord tone:

Example E

Exercise 5

1. The chords shown in this exercise (C, D, G minor, and A minor) are the only major or minor triads that can be derived from the C Lixian scale: C D E F♯ G A B♭ (see Chapter 5).

2. Write a small theme based on these chords.

3. Use chord tones or reverse neighboring tones (label them "r.n.t."). The reverse neighboring tones must belong to the C Lixian scale and be no longer than a ¼ note.

An *escaped tone* is a non-chord tone that moves from a chord tone by skip and proceeds to another chord tone by skip. It has escaped from the chord and is the *hottest* form of non-chord tone, particularly when it is nondiatonic (as in *c* in the following example):

Example F

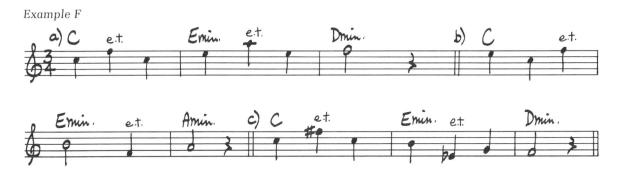

Exercise 6

1. Compose a small theme based on the chords given, which are in D Dorian.

2. Use only chord tones and escaped tones (label these "e.t."). The escaped tones are not restricted to tones of the D Dorian scale. They must not be longer than a ¼ note.

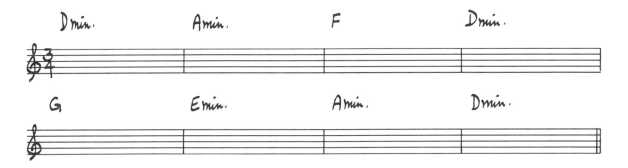

> *Hint:* A non-chord tone should never be longer than a ¼ note in moderate 4/4. This applies especially to nondiatonic non-chord tones and to changing tones, escaped tones, and reverse neighboring tones, all three of which tend to cloud the harmony.

DIATONIC NON-3RD CHORDS

Early in this chapter I introduced chords constructed of intervals other than 3rds. These chords are called *non-3rd chords*; even though they may contain 3rds, they are not built exclusively of 3rds.

Example G shows chords built entirely of 4ths, 5ths, and 2nds—using tones only from the C major scale. Chords built of 2nds, or mostly of 2nds, are called *clusters*. Play those chords and get a feeling for their uniqueness.

Example G

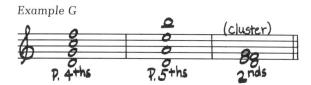

The non-3rd chords below are not made up solely of one interval, but use a variety of intervals:

Example H

Exercise 7

Label the intervals in these non-3rd chords:

Exercise 8

1. Using only the tones of the C major scale, write several non-3rd chords of three to five tones each.
2. Label the intervals used in these chords. (Remember, you may use 3rds, but you may not construct chords *exclusively* of 3rds.)
3. Play these chords slowly several times.

Hint: Some chords look like non-3rd chords but they are really triads. When the chord in Example I, *a*, is redistributed, it is equivalent to the C major triad in *b*; when the chord in *c* is redistributed, it becomes *d*, a four-tone chord made up exclusively of 3rds.

Example I

Exercise 9

1. Write an oom-pah or oom-pah-pah accompaniment of eight to twelve measures for piano in the bass clef, below, based on non-3rd chords of two to four tones each, diatonic to the C major scale. Begin and end on the same chord.

2. Use one chord for one or two measures.

3. You may have to redistribute the chords to make them flow more smoothly and be easier to play.

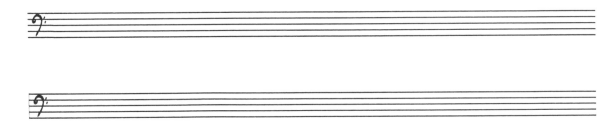

Exercise 10

(Do Exercise 9 first!)

1. In the treble clef, below, compose a melody to the accompaniment you wrote for Exercise 9. Use "chord tones" only. Use transformational processes and label them.

2. Since this melody is based on the C major scale accompaniment constructed for Exercise 9, it will be made up entirely of tones in the C major scale.

3. Refer to the General Rules that are applicable, here and in all exercises.

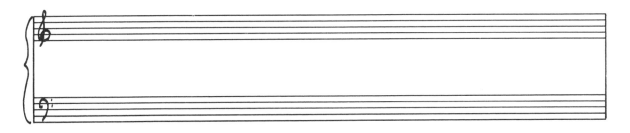

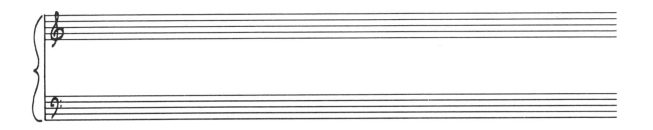

Another technique is to construct a new harmonic world out of three or four diatonic non-3rd chords that you can move to and from freely, as shown in Example J: One such chord should be the tonic chord (home base), and one or two of the others should push back home to the tonic. Play these four chords in different sequences, and redistribute them too, occasionally adding octave forms of one or two tones to the chord position:

Example J

DERIVING NON-3RD CHORDS
FROM A DIATONIC MELODY

Sometimes we reverse the procedure seen in Exercises 9 and 10, and we derive the chords from the melody. The melody in Example K is composed of tones from the C major scale; they center around the tone A, which becomes the tonic. The chords, stated in the form of oom-pah, are made up of tones from the melody; they do not contain these few tones marked with crosses, which should be thought of as non-chord tones. Note that the chords in measures 2 and 6 contain tones from measures 1 and 5 respectively, and that all of the chords are made up of three tones, except for the last chord, which has only two tones:

Example K

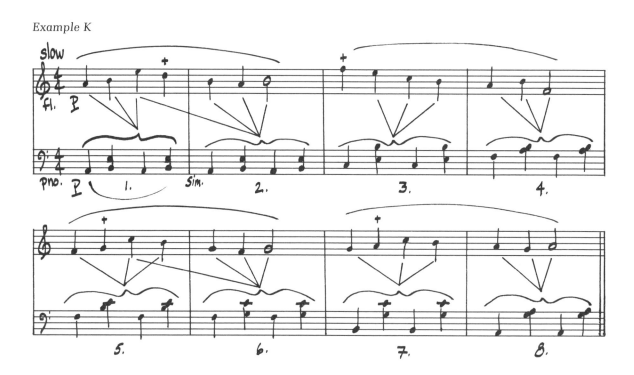

Exercise 11

1. Compose a melody of six to nineteen measures in the treble clef; use only the tones of the C major scale, centering on the F or G. The tone you choose should be thought of as the tonic, and you should begin and end your melody on this tone.

2. Derive non-3rd chords from this melody according to the procedures shown in Example K and then construct a repeated-chord accompaniment from these chords. Your first chord must have the tonic as its lowest tone, and if possible it should also be used as your last chord, even if its tones are not in the melody at that point.

3. Use lines and brackets to show chord derivation, as in Example K.

Of course, you may also derive *3rd* chords from diatonic melodies, and you may derive a *mixture* of 3rd and non-3rd chords from diatonic melodies—in any of the twelve keys. This is a subject I can only touch on here.

These procedures—composing melodies and chords that are restricted to one key—are often referred to as "white-note fever." I like these procedures, and urge you to use them, but this uncharitable phrase will perhaps remind you of the excesses to which they can lead.

DERIVING CHORDS FROM NONDIATONIC MELODIES

The procedure of deriving chords from melody is also applicable to *nondiatonic* melody, as Example L shows. Note that (1) the chords move one to the measure; (2) tones not included in the chord are a ¼ note or less in duration; and (3) tones not in the chord move by major or minor 2nd to ones that are included in the chord.

Example L

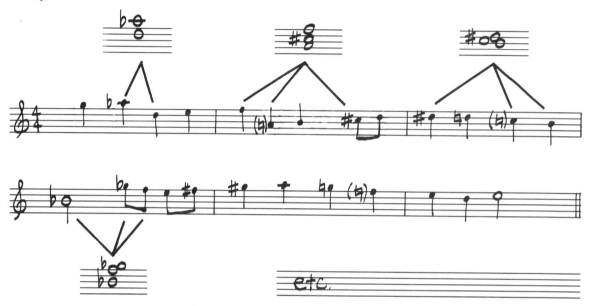

Exercise 12

Derive new chords from this same melody (which is written out again in this exercise), using the procedures just discussed. Then compose an accompaniment based on these chords.

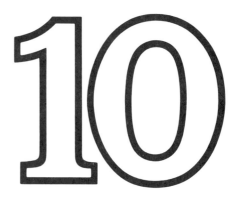

Counterpoint

1:1 COUNTERPOINT
AND CONSONANT INTERVALS

Counterpoint consists of two or more melodies sounded at the same time. The simplest form of counterpoint is made up of two melodies with identical rhythms. This is called one-to-one counterpoint (or 1:1 counterpoint).

When the notes are of long duration, the intervals between the two melodies (or *parts,* as they are called in counterpoint) should be "consonant." The consonant intervals are:

> perfect unison
> perfect octave
> perfect fourth
> perfect fifth
> major or minor third
> major or minor sixth

In the music, the intervals are labeled by number:

Example A

Exercise 1

Construct consonant intervals above or below each of the following tones and label each interval:

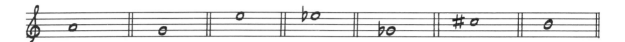

Example B shows 1:1 two-part counterpoint in C Lixian. Even though the two melodies have identical rhythms, each has its own curve and is modestly independent of the other. In measure 4, note that the intervals of a 10th and a 12th are labeled as 3rd and 5th; this is the common procedure for intervals larger than an octave.

Example B

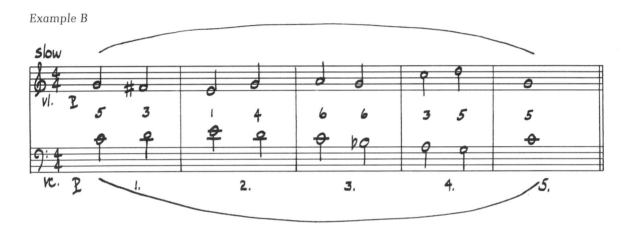

TYPES OF MOVEMENT BETWEEN VOICES

Movement from one interval to another has four classifications: *parallel motion* (a in Example C)—both parts moving in one direction by the same interval; *similar motion* (b)—two parts moving in the same direction, but not by identical intervals; *oblique motion* (c and d)—one part remaining on the same tone while the other moves up or down; and *contrary motion* (e and f)—two parts moving in opposite directions.

Example C

All four classifications of movement in Example C are usable, although you should note that the parts will have more independence with oblique and contrary motion than with parallel and similar motion; two parts in parallel 3rds from beginning to end will sound more like harmony than counterpoint. This is not to say that parallel and similar motion are to be avoided, but that they are less like counterpoint. (See Chapter 11 for a fuller discussion of two or more parallel parts.)

There are a few formations that definitely should be avoided, and they all involve the perfect unison and the perfect octave. These two intervals tend to stand out excessively in two-part counterpoint and consequently need to be treated with care: successive octaves (*a*, in Example D), successive unisons (*b*), and similar motion from any interval to a unison or octave (*c*). However, all these formations are acceptable as the last two intervals of a section of a piece.

Example D

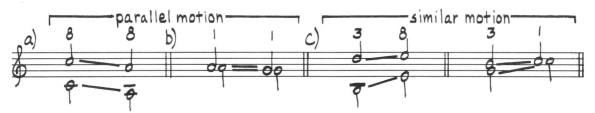

THREE 1:1 EXERCISES

Exercise 2

1. Complete the melody in the treble clef with tones from D Dorian. Use only those tones that form consonant intervals with the corresponding tones in the bass clef. Label each interval.

2. Avoid similar or parallel motion to a unison or octave, except to the last interval.

3. Refer to the General Rules that are applicable, here and in all exercises.

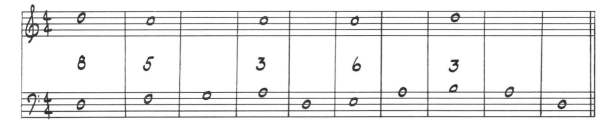

Exercise 3

1. Compose a melody in the bass clef, duplicating the rhythm of the melody in the treble clef.

2. The melody in the treble clef is centered around the tone G, but it is not limited to any one key or scale. The new melody must be centered around the tone G and does not need to conform to any key or scale either.

3. Each tone of the new melody must form a consonant interval with the corresponding tone in the treble-clef melody.

4. Avoid similar or parallel motion to a unison or octave, except to the last interval.

5. The treble-clef melody is a small-theme form (a b a c); duplicate this form in the bass-clef melody if you wish.

Exercise 4

1. Compose two-part 1:1 counterpoint (using identical rhythms and consonant intervals only) six to twelve measures long in the space provided. Label each interval.

2. Use the two scales shown. These scales are built on different tones; using them together results in *bitonality*—the process of using two tonalities at once. The tonality of the *lower* scale will predominate. Use the tones of the E Phrygian scale in the treble clef:

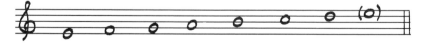

Use the tones of the C Lixian scale in the bass clef:

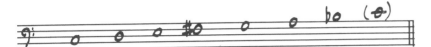

3. Be sure to use *all* of the tones in these two scales so that the character of each is revealed and the contrast between the two is evident.

4. Use only these three rhythms:

5. Try for repetitions and sequences, not only within each voice but *between* the two voices as well.

2:1 COUNTERPOINT

Now let us turn to two-to-one counterpoint—two tones in one part to one tone in the other parts, as shown in Example E. Note that the ½ note has an intervalic relationship with *both* ¼ notes and that all the intervals are consonant:

Example E

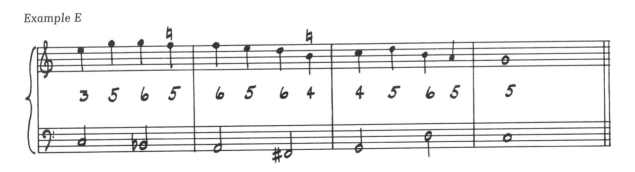

Four formations to be avoided in two-part 2:1 counterpoint (except to the last interval of the section or piece) are:

Example F

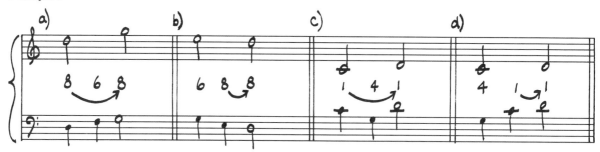

Exercise 5

1. In the bass clef, compose a melody of ¼ notes using the tones of the C Dorian scale (C D E♭ F G A B♭). The given melody, in the treble clef, is in E Phrygian.

2. Each interval formed between the two parts must be consonant. Label each interval.

3. Avoid the formations shown in Example F.

Example G is a "mistake" example. Play it at the piano and try to find the mistakes before you look at the mistake list below.

Example G

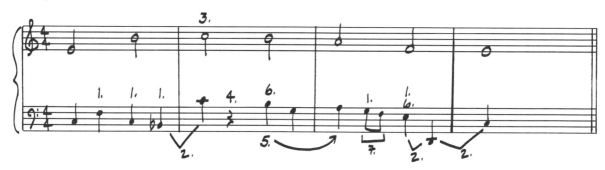

   Mistake List

1. Not a consonant interval.
2. Unsingable skip.

3. Similar motion to an octave.
4. Rest not permitted.
5. A form of parallel octaves.
6. A tone not in C Dorian.
7. ⅛th notes (not permitted).

(Also note that the bass clef part exceeds the range of a 10th.)

All intervals other than consonant intervals can be thought of as *dissonant* intervals. These may be used in 2:1 *two-part* counterpoint if they move by major or minor 2nd to a tone that forms a consonant interval with the other part:

Example H

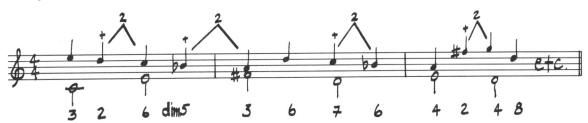

Exercise 6

1. Compose a ¼ note melody in the treble clef in E Phrygian, using both consonant and dissonant intervals, as shown in Example H.
2. Try for occasional repetitions and sequences.
3. Label all intervals and mark the dissonant intervals with a cross.

Exercise 7

1. Compose 2:1 two-part counterpoint six to ten measures long according to the procedures developed in this chapter. Use repetitions and sequences occasionally.

2. Use only the tones of the blues scale: (E G A B♭ B D).

TWO-PART COUNTERPOINT WITH CHORDS

Up to this point, we have dealt with counterpoint *intervalically*—from one interval to another. Counterpoint may also be thought of *harmonically*, as seen in Example I, which consists entirely of chord tones. In counterpoint with harmony, let us assume that a multiple-note instrument, such as piano or guitar, states the chords; this relieves us from the responsibility of representing the harmony through the counterpoint, which is another topic altogether and one that goes far beyond the scope of this book. Example I is written in C Dorian (C D E♭ F G A B♭), for which you may use the key signature of B♭ major (the Dorian scale is built on the second tone of a major scale) or write in the flat signs, as I have done:

Example I

Exercise 8

1. Compose a melody of ½ notes only, made up exclusively of chord tones. (Note that this exercise is in C Phrygian: C D♭ E♭ F G A♭ B♭.)

2. Note that all the intervals so formed will be consonant.

3. Label all the intervals, which will help you to see that they are all consonant.

4. Avoid similar motion to a unison or octave, except to the last interval.

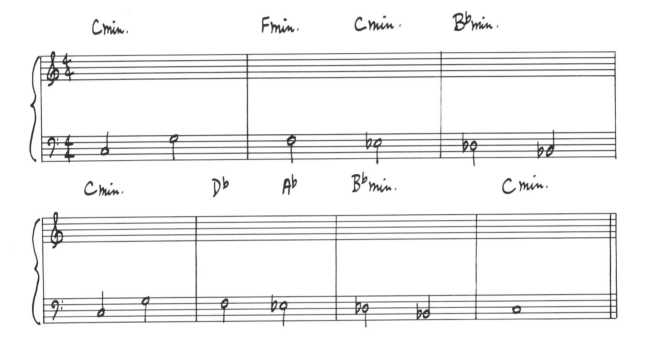

In composing 2:1 two-part counterpoint, you may use chord tones and non-chord tones. The non-chord tones should be a duration of a ¼ note or less (in moderate 3/4 or 4/4) and may include passing tones, neighboring tones, auxiliary tones, and anticipation tones:

Example J

Sometimes the non-chord tone forms a consonant interval with the other part; it should still be treated as a non-chord tone:

Example K

Two-part 2:1 counterpoint may also be composed with the ¼ notes in the treble and then in the bass, and so on:

Example L

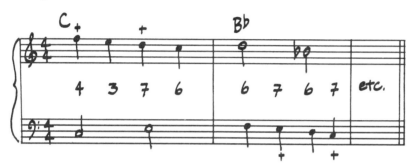

Exercise 9

1. Compose a melody in the treble clef using chord tones, passing tones, neighboring tones, auxiliary tones, and anticipation tones—never two in succession. Label the non-chord tones.

2. Use ¼ notes when the given melody is made up of ½ notes, and vice versa. End with a whole note.

3. Note the motives in the given bass melody and try to use sequences and repetitions in the treble clef also.

4. Refer to the General Rules that are applicable, here and in all exercises.

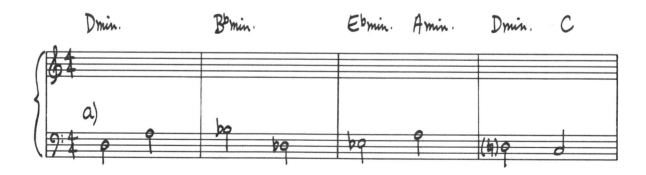

TWO-PART COUNTERPOINT
AND THE PENTATONIC SCALE

The chart in Example M shows the intervalic relationships between all the tones in the E pentatonic scale. Note that of the ten possible relationships, seven are consonant and only three are dissonant:

Example M

The relatively small number of dissonant intervals in the pentatonic scale suggests that it lends itself readily to two-part counterpoint.

Exercise 10

1. Compose 2:1 two-part counterpoint ten to twenty measures long, using only the tones of the E pentatonic scale.

2. Avoid similar and parallel motion to a unison or octave, except as a closing formation.

3. Use repetitions and sequences, within each part and between the parts.

4. Use only ¼ notes and ½ notes.
5. Label all the intervals formed between the parts.

The pentatonic scale also lends itself well to 3:1 and 4:1 counterpoint, and also to counterpoint in which there is no rhythmic ratio between the parts. It is also relatively easy to write good counterpoint of more than two parts with the pentatonic scale. These topics are beyond the scope of this book, except for some isolated examples to be found in Chapter 16.

CONTRAPUNTAL ASPECTS OF MELODY AND ACCOMPANIMENT

Although the relationship between melody and accompaniment is not counterpoint as such, it is like counterpoint in some ways: the ear hears the melody as one part and the accompaniment as another part or parts. The chief concern for us in this relationship is similar and parallel motion to a unison or octave, as seen in Example N. The parallel octaves between the melody and the accompaniment in *a* are better avoided; *b* is the preferred version.

Example N

The thinly disguised parallel octaves in *a* are also to be avoided; *b* is a distinct improvement:

Example O

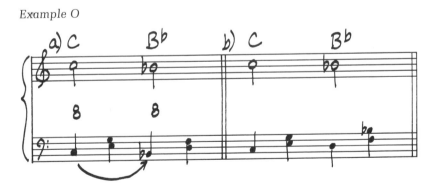

When you listen to melody with harmonic accompaniment, your ear hears the *outside* tones first and most clearly. In a passage like the one shown in Example P, your ear hears the highest tone (the melody tone) and the lowest tone (the lowest tone of the chord) more immediately and more clearly than the other tones; consequently, there is a special relationship between the outside tones. The parallel octaves in *a* should be avoided in favor of the distribution in *b*:

Example P

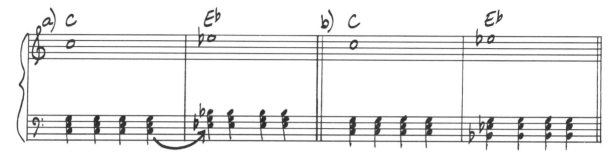

One very general rule is to be careful with *all* octave formations that occur at the beginning of the measure since these formations tend to draw too much attention to themselves. It is always satisfactory to end a piece or section, of course, with an octave built on the tonic.

Organum

TWO VOICES IN ORGANUM

Organum is the name for two or more voices traveling the same road—locked together in the same rhythm and moving by the same interval. In Example A the lower part exactly duplicates the upper part a perfect 5th below:

Example A

Example B is also organum: the lower part duplicates the melody a major 3rd below, which results in parallel major 3rds. In measure 2, note that the lower part has a D♭ and the upper part a D♮; conflicting accidentals often occur when two parts share the same staff, especially in organum. You must be careful to write exactly what you mean.

Example B

Exercise 1

1. To the given melody, write a lower part built a perfect 4th below.

2. Use downward stems for the lower part.

3. Refer to the General Rules that are applicable, here and in all exercises.

Exercise 2

1. Write a lower part a major 3rd below the given melody, using downward stems.

2. Be sure of your accidentals, not only in the added part but in the given melody as well (see measure 2).

Organum between dissonant intervals can be "sweetened" by wide spacing, as shown below in Example C.

Example C

116

Exercise 3

1. In the organum below, the lower part was supposed to be a major 9th below the upper melody, but a lot of mistakes crept in. Circle each mistake and correct it. Correct only the *lower* part and leave the upper melody alone.

Exercise 4

1. To the given melody write a lower part a minor 7th below.

2. Write this exercise out in two ways: first write it on separate staffs and then on one staff.

3RD CHORDS IN ORGANUM

It is possible to have organum with more than two voices. Example D consists of organum in three voices. The second part is a minor 3rd below the melody (the top part), and the third part is

117

a major 3rd below the second part. The result, of course, is a series of major triads in exactly the same position. Play this example very slowly and note its richness.

Example D

Exercise 5

The melody is on the top staff below. The second part is in organum a minor 3rd below the melody. Add a third part a major 3rd below the second part, on the third staff.

In Example E, *a*, the second part is a perfect 4th below the melody, and the third part is a minor 3rd below the second part. Sometimes it is desirable to open up this kind of organum chord, as in Example E, *b*, where the second part of *a* has been dropped an octave and becomes the third part. (You can also think of this in another way: the second part is a minor 6th below the given melody, and the third part is a major 6th below the second part.)

Example E

118

Exercise 6

1. The melody is on the top staff.
2. Write the second part in organum a perfect 5th below on the second staff.
3. Write the third part on the third staff a minor 6th below the second part.
4. Choose three brass instruments (or any three available instruments that are suitable) for this passage.

Exercise 7

1. Compose a melody using the E blues scale (see Chapter 5) on the top staff.
2. Do not exceed the range of an octave.
3. Write organum with the melody as the top part, using all major or all minor triads. (Do not mix them: use either major *or* minor.)
4. Write these either in "close position," as in Example E, *a*, or "open position," as in Example E, *b*.

NON-3RD CHORDS IN ORGANUM

Non-3rd chords may also be used in organum. In Example F the second part is a perfect 5th below the given melody and the third part is a major 9th below the second part.

Example F

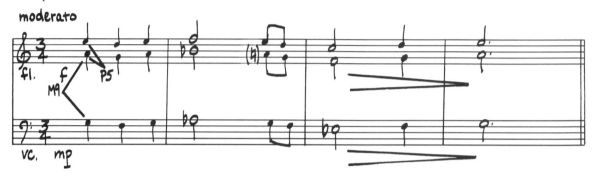

Exercise 8

1. Continue the process of organum shown in the first measure of *a*.

2. Write this organum in *reduced* form as well: put the two treble-clef parts on one staff and place the bass-clef part on the lower staff, as in *b*.

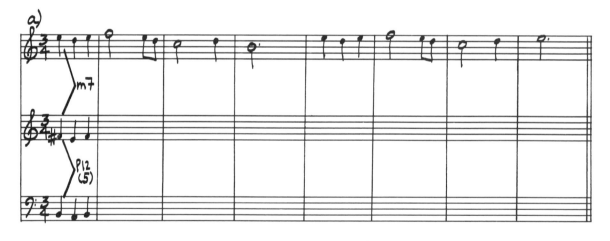

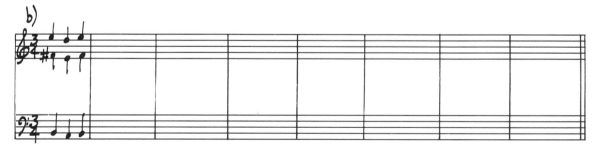

Exercise 9

1. Compose a melody of ten to twenty measures in length that seems to describe an old man, after he's had a little wine, dancing at his granddaughter's wedding.

2. Use only the scale of C ditonic. Start and end on the same tone and use a total range of an octave or less.

3. Employ only these rhythms:

4. Construct a juicy four-tone non-3rd chord for the first tone of this melody (this chord may contain tones other than those in the C ditonic scale) and continue this chord in organum for the course of the melody. It is generally wise to use larger intervals between the lower voices of such a chord; you will find that an interval smaller than a 5th in the lower voices will usually sound muddy.

5. Using separate manuscript paper for this assignment, write this organum on four staffs, assigning each to an appropriate instrument. Put each instrument in an easy, comfortable part of its range.

6. Transcribe this piece in reduced form also; use one or two staffs, as needed. And watch out for accidentals! (See Exercise 8.)

ORGANUM AS A SOURCE

Organum can also be used to *generate* entire pieces. Example G shows such a piece. It is a short piece for two instruments in which the lower instrument is used only in organum with the upper instrument. Note the richness of the organum passages in contrast to the solo passages. (Also note the natural signs in measures 11, 14, and 15; these tell the trumpet player not to worry about the conflicting sharps in the trombone part.)

Example G

122

Exercise 10

Analyze the *form* of the trumpet part in Example G according to the procedures of small-form construction outlined in Chapter 4. Use capital letters and lower-case letters.

Exercise 11

1. Compose a small theme of eight to twelve measures in length using the blues scale.

2. Use organum procedures to write a second part lower than the first for another instrument. Use any interval for the second part and stick to it. Use your ears.

Example H (not based entirely on Basic Note Values) shows how a small theme consisting of eight measures can be made into a short piece of twenty-six measures by means of organum:

1. Measures 1–8 make up the small theme, which is divided between the clarinet and the bassoon.

2. Measures 9—12 show an organum of the lower 6th. Notice that the organum is *inexact*; some of the 6ths are major and some are minor, in accordance with the tones of the D Dorian scale.

3. Measures 13—14 are in octaves.

4. Measures 15—16 show the bassoon in perfect 5ths (12ths actually) below the melody.

5. Measures 17–20 show an added part *above* the melody; the clarinet moves in parallel major 3rds (10ths, actually) above the bassoon.

6. Measures 21–22 show the clarinet a major 6th above the melody.

7. Measures 23–24 show the melody (played by the clarinet) in a higher octave with an added part a minor 7th below.

8. Measures 25–26 are "free measures," in which reference is made to the original motive and the piece is rounded off.

Example H

Exercise 12

1. Compose a small theme based on the C ditonic scale.
2. Apply the procedures shown in Example H by extending this small theme as far as you can. Use three available instruments.
3. Write on separate manuscript paper and use three staves.

ORGANUM AS ACCOMPANIMENT

An excellent way to use organum is for accompaniment. Parallel 5ths played by bass guitar are often heard in rock and roll. For example:

Example I

Example J shows parallel 5ths that will become an accompaniment later. Note that the passage forms an *a a* (the second *a* is slightly altered at the end):

Example J

Using this same organum accompaniment, I have composed a melody compatible with it in the treble clef. The melody consists of tones found in the organum (think of these as "chord tones" even though there is no "chord," strictly speaking) and non-chord tones (these are labeled the first time they occur). Note that I use non-chord tones of a ¼ note's duration or less and that measures 4 and 8 contain a reverse neighboring tone, a variety of non-chord tone that requires great delicacy to use.

126

Example K

Exercise 13

1. Compose a new melody to this same organum, which has been written out again below.

2. Use only tones from the organum and non-chord tones of a ¼ note's value or less. These should be labeled with a cross.

In Example L I have constructed an organum of minor triads in the bass clef as an accompaniment and I have composed a melody in the treble clef using chord tones and non-chord tones. Note that the *c* is derived from the *a*, which gives these eight measures a sense of *a b a b*.

Example L

Exercise 14

1. Construct a chordal organum (all major or all minor triads) four measures in length using long-value notes only (½ notes and whole notes) in the bass clef.

2. Compose a melody (A) based on chord tones and non-chord tones (none longer than a ¼ note) four measures long.

3. Then compose a contrasting melody (B) to the same organum (as in step 2), one that wants to return to the first melody (A).

4. Then repeat the first melody, resulting in ABA.

5. Write this all out on separate manuscript paper. Use four separate staffs, one for the melody and one each for the three parts of the organum triad. Be sure that your melody has plenty of elbow room and that it stays away from the tones in the organum chords, whether it is above or below the organum.

en examined more thoroughly
because the procedures of
. Other material in this book
d you might very well decide
example, it would be easy to
d on the material concerning
ells (see Chapter 7), especially
om time to time.

Imitation: a Useful Game

THE GAME

A few years ago, when I was the director of the Chicago Free Theater, I invented a game for percussion instruments. It is a very simple game, and here are the rules.

1. Three, four, or five players stand in a circle.
2. Each player has a hand-held percussion instrument.
3. When the group is ready to begin, one of the players introduces a simple figuration of one or two measures. This figuration must clearly suggest the tempo and must have *shape*, so that it can be recalled easily.
4. During the course of the piece, each player may *introduce one* such figuration (and only one).
5. Each player may *imitate* any of the figurations (his or others) at any time (and not necessarily consecutively).
6. Each player may *rest* at any time (remember: silence is music).
7. The piece may end either by a signal from one of the players or by a group consensus that the piece has finished.

This game, which I call "Imitation" because of rule 5 above, is a very useful way to learn how to pass material from one instrument to another. Using only simple one-measure figurations, I have written an example of how a piece evolved from these rules might sound. Play this, if you are in a class:

Example A

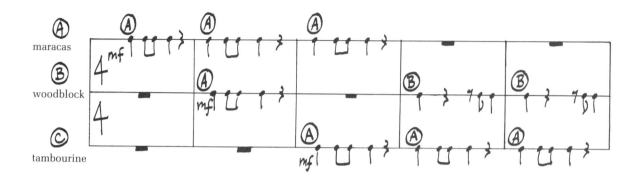

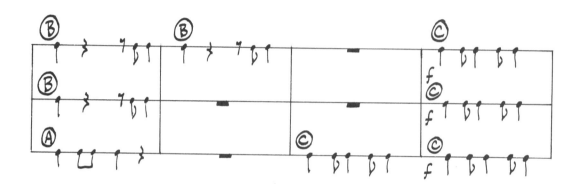

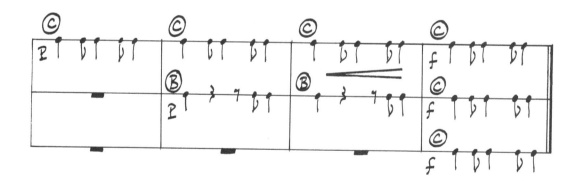

If the players are careless about the rules and lack a sense of the whole, they might perform something like Example B where several mistakes are evident:

Example B

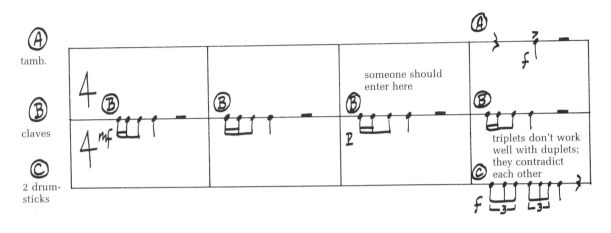

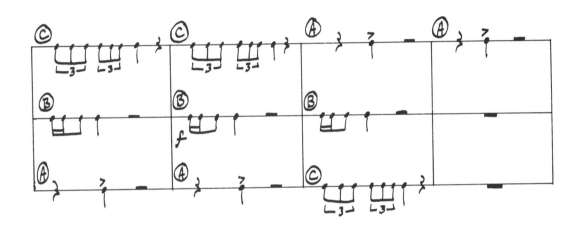

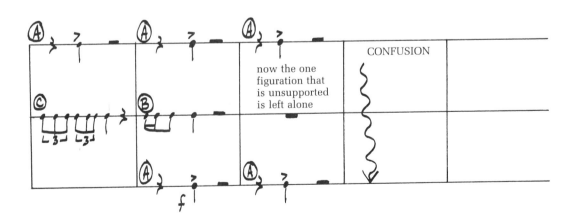

Also note that player A (tambourine) never lets up—he starts in measure 4 and then plays in every measure.

Exercise 1 (for three players)

Improvise a piece based on the rules of Imitation (as given above), using three hand-held percussion instruments that are available to you. Use one-measure and two-measure figurations and avoid figurations that are hard to imitate or that are unsupported (more about this later). Listen carefully to one another and don't try to be stars.

Figuration B in Example C is an isolated example of an unsupported figuration that works well when played at the same time as A but not so well when it is played by itself. When played by itself it does not give a sense of the tempo or of the shape of the measure:

Example C

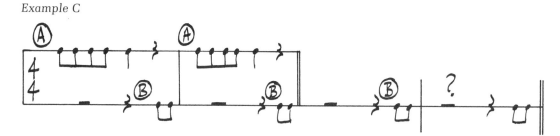

Exercise 2

Now you should be able to compose a piece based on the game. Use three available percussion instruments, follow the rules, and avoid the pitfalls. Refer to the General Rules that are applicable. Label *each* use of A, B, and C.

Ⓐ

Ⓑ

Ⓒ

IMITATION WITH MELODY

In Example D the process of Imitation is applied to pitch as well as to rhythm. Each instrument has the same two pitches. (When Imitation is played as a game, the players decide which pitches to use before starting.) Notice the frequent whole-measure rests.

Example D

Exercise 3

1. Compose a short piece for three available instruments based
   on the principles of Imitation. Use only these three figurations, each of which may be transposed to another octave (in
   whole, not in part). Note that these figurations are made up
   of a "frictionless" cell (see Chapter 7 and Chapter 10):

2. Give each instrument elbow room (see Chapter 8) and use
   frequent whole-measure rests.

3. To bring the piece to a close, you may use one or two free
   measures, in which you are not restricted to the three figurations (but you must use only E, A, and B in the free measures).

4. Label each figuration each time that it appears.

5. Refer to the General Rules that are applicable, here and in all
   exercises.

Hint: Usually any tone of a cell may be its tonic. It is important
for you to find and maintain the tonic.

OVERLAPPING

When you use two-measure figurations, the possibility of *overlapping* occurs—that is, the imitation of a two-measure figuration might begin before the figuration is complete, as in measure 4 of Example E.

Example E

Exercise 4

1. Develop three two-measure figurations using the cell E B D in any octave.

2. Compose a piece of about one minute's length based on the rules of Imitation using only these three figurations. Write for three instruments.

3. You may transpose these figurations to other octaves (in whole, not in part), and you may use the overlapping procedure seen in Example E.

4. Give each instrument elbow room and use frequent whole-measure rests.

5. If you wish, you may use one or two free measures to bring the piece to a close, still using only the cell.

6. Write this piece out on separate manuscript paper.

FRAGMENTATION

When a portion of a one- or two-measure figuration is *palpable*, you may separate it from the main figuration and use it by itself. By a *palpable portion*, I mean a portion that makes sense by itself, that is easily identified by the ear, and that bears repetition. In Example F both the first and second measures are palpable portions; note how the second measure can be separated from the first:

Example F

Here is how such *fragmentation* of a figuration might be worked
into an Imitation piece:

Example G

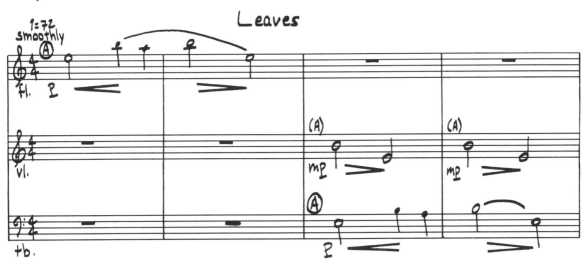

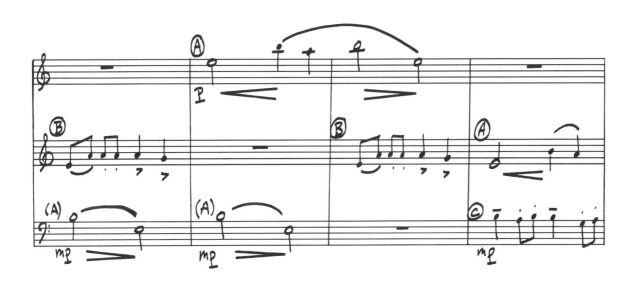

Exercise 5

1. Develop four one-to-two measure figurations using only the tones of the E pentatonic scale: E G A B D.

2. Compose a piece that is two to three minutes in duration based on the rules of Imitation, using only these four figurations or palpable portions of them, for four instruments. The intervals between the five tones of the pentatonic scale contain only three dissonances, and these are mild dissonances (see Example M, Chapter 10). In other words, you will be able to deal with the vertical tensions (dissonances) in this piece by judicious use of your ear.

3. The last one or two measures of the piece may be freely composed with tones from the E pentatonic scale.

4. Give the instruments elbow room and be sure to use frequent whole-measure rests. Let plenty of air into this piece.

5. Use separate manuscript paper.

TAKING RISKS WITH IMITATION

The pentatonic scale, like other cells used in this chapter, is relatively free of vertical tensions, as you should know very well by now. In the cell shown in Example H on the other hand, the vertical tensions are quite pronounced:

Example H

Exercise 6

Label all the intervalic relationships in Example H: first tone to second tone, first to third, and so forth. Use the space below.

Despite the large number of dissonant intervals in the cell in Example H, it is nonetheless an abundant source of figurations that have a viable contrapuntal relationship, such as the ones in Example I:

Example I

Exercise 7

Construct two figurations from the cell in Example H that fit each other in 1:1 or 2:1 (non-chordal) two-part counterpoint:

(See Chapter 10, Exercise 4, in which counterpoint between two different *scales* is discussed.)

It is also possible to achieve good counterpoint (according to the rules in Chapter 10) between two different cells. The two cells in Example J share one tone, G:

Example J

Example K shows two figurations derived from the two cells in Example J that follow the rules of two-part counterpoint. This example is chiefly 1:1, except for two points that are 2:1 (marked with asterisks):

Example K

Note that the first interval forms a minor 6th *enharmonically*, which is permitted in counterpoint based on cells and rows but is to be avoided elsewhere.

Exercise 8

1. Compose a short piece based on the principles of Imitation for three available instruments. Use only the two figurations in Example K, each of which may be transposed to another octave (in whole, not in part). Use separate manuscript paper.

2. You may use a palpable portion of one of the figurations by itself or *with the corresponding portion of the other figuration.*

3. Give each instrument elbow room and use frequent whole-measure rests.

4. You may not use free measures at the end of the piece.

5. Label each figuration each time it appears.

6. Refer to the General Rules that are applicable, here and in all exercises.

13

Words
and Music

THE PREMISE

This chapter deals with the relationship between words and music. Using only the materials available to you in this book, I shall attempt to show you how to put words and music together and how to start a song.

I base the procedures outlined here on the songs and arias of Mozart, Schubert, and Verdi among the classical masters and of George Gershwin, Richard Rodgers, and Cole Porter among the popular masters—with one exception, which is *melisma*, used by the classical masters. Melisma is the use of more than one tone for one syllable. (Please sing all the examples in this chapter.)

Example A

Melisma is used very frequently in classical music. In addition to showing off the beauty of the human voice, it allows the composer to *regularize* lines that are irregular. For example, if the first line has four syllables and the second line has three syllables, the composer is able to use the same four tone motive for both lines by writing two tones for one syllable in the second line:

Example B

However, I feel that melisma gets in the way of understanding the words and it provides easy ways out of problems that you should learn to solve without its use, so I have excluded it here.

TEXT AND LYRICS

The usual name for words set to music is *text*. In popular music, the words of a song are called the *lyrics*. As a general rule, in classical music the text is written before the music; in popular music the music often comes first. Give and take between the word writer and the music writer is often possible, and, of course, there are many different ways of writing a song. In teaching this subject, it is more practical if the words come first, and therefore this is the approach we will use.

Before going further, I want to point out some important differences between text and poetry (especially the kind of text found in the work of Gershwin and other popular composers). The following list should help you understand these differences:

Sung Words	*Poetry (especially of the Twentieth Century)*
Short lines of regular length	Long and short lines irregularly mixed
Short words, often of one syllable	Long as well as short words
Short sentences and phrases, which usually correspond with the line	Sometimes very long sentences and phrases (even extending the entire length of the poem) often not corresponding with the lines at all
A regular rhythm in the line, sometimes extending over the entire lyric	Irregular rhythm
Simple, concise thoughts	Abstract thoughts, sometimes expressed at great length

Frequent repetition of words and phrases meant to be heard	Infrequent repetition of words and phrases often read silently
Words and groups of words that are easily spoken	Words and groups of words that are sometime spoken with difficulty
Perfect rhymes ("best"/"rest")	Perfect rhymes and imperfect rhymes ("time"/"fine") and look-alikes ("gone"/"lone")

In short, *song texts* are written to be heard—and heard without time to reflect on complex lines or phrases. To make this clear, here are two examples written by my long-time collaborator Jon Swan. First is an example of words written to be sung:

Example C

> *Nothing's big as mama.*
> *Take a look at me.*
> *Nothing's big as mama.*
> *Take a look at me.*
> *Nothing's big as mama.*
> *Just you wait and see!*

And here is the first stanza of a poem, "Conjuring Blues in the Surf at Nantucket" by Jon Swan:

Example D

> *There are no bluefish. Only*
> *stories about bluefish. Like unicorns they thrive*
> *in the imagination, the mother-wit sea*
> *out of which we stepped originally,*
> *not this one we drive*
> *to each evening. We park the car on the bluff.*
> *We take our shoes off.*
> *Holding long rods, we walk down*
> *to the dividing line between two kingdoms to join*
> *the other dreamers*
> *already casting their lures.*

Your job as a composer is to find melody and harmony that reflect the character or meaning of a text and at the same time make the meaning clear to the listener. Although you may be tempted to highlight an unimportant word or distort a meaning for the sake of a good melody you must resist this urge, and find a good melody that works with the words.

THE RHYTHM OF THE WORDS

There is rhythm in a line of text and in poetry. This rhythm comes from the way you would speak such a line—the *normal accenting* of the syllables in a line. In Example E accented syllables are marked " — ," and unaccented syllables are marked " ◡ ." Say these words aloud and see if the marks are adequate:

Example E

Oh, what fun to run a-way,
Oh, what joy to be a-lone.
How nice to say good-bye.

Exercise 1

Place the marks for accented and unaccented syllables below each syllable in these two lines (as in Example E):

Be-neath the wa-ters of the sea
Are lob-sters thick as thick can be.

DURATION

One of the best ways to express the rhythm of a line is through *duration*; long notes are given to accented syllables and short notes to unaccented syllables. Read the words in Example F aloud in tempo (this is called *chant*). Only two note values are used—¼ notes and ½ notes.

Example F

Oh, what fun to run a-way,

Example G is loaded with mistakes; it goes against the normal accents of the words and against the meaning of the lines. Chant it to see what I mean:

Example G

Oh, what fun to run a-way,

Oh, what joy to be a-lone.

Exercise 2

1. Find the normal rhythm of the following lines by speaking them aloud several times.
2. Mark each syllable with — or ⏝ below it.
3. Set the words as chant, using ½ notes for the accented syllables and ¼ notes for the unaccented syllables; place these notes *above* the syllables.

If a man is not a fool,

He will talk of life with love.

PITCH

In addition to duration, another important consideration in setting words is *pitch*—the choice of tones for a given syllable. Using a two-tone cell, I have set the following line with ¼ notes only. Note that the accented syllables are given the higher tone and the unaccented syllables are given the lower tone. Remember to sing all these examples.

Example H

Exercise 3

Set the given words with A and C, using only ¼ notes. Give the accented syllables the upper tones, and vice versa. Do not use bar lines.

Example I uses two pitches and two durations. The accented syllables are set with the upper tone and the longer duration, and vice versa.

Example I

Example I is not entirely satisfactory; it is true that "Oh," "fun," "run," and "-way" are the accented syllables, but "Oh" is far less important than the other three. With two pitches and two durations, distinctions between important and less important accented syllables can be made:

Example J

Exercise 4

1. Set the given words with the tones A and C.
2. Use only ½ notes and ¼ notes, without bar lines.
3. Set *all* the accented syllables with the upper tone, but give ½-note duration only to accented syllables in *important* words.

Using a 3-tone cell and ¼ notes is another way to find the normal accent of the line while at the same time presenting the distinction between important and less important words, as Example K shows. (Also, bear in mind that identical groups of words may have different meanings, according to the context, and that your job is to find the meaning that is most nearly correct.)

Example K

Here is another example of three *pitches* and one duration; as you can see, it works badly:

Example L

Exercise 5

Set the given words as in Example K.

How nice to say good - bye.

Example M uses three pitches and two durations, which permit even more varied ways of putting words and music together. Note that "Oh," a relatively unimportant accented syllable, is given the lowest of three tones but a longer duration. Note that "what," an unimportant word, is given the middle tone, with a ¼-note duration, rather than the lowest tone.

Example M

Oh, what fun to run a-way.

Exercise 6

Set the given words as in Example M.

No-thing's big as ma - ma. Take a look at me.

THE BAR LINE

Now let us discuss the *bar line*. A series of ¼ notes will inevitably be performed with a slightly greater emphasis given to the first ¼ note in each measure:

Example N

Consequently, if the duration of each syllable is the same, the syllable following the bar line will receive more accent than the others. (And in 4/4 the third ¼ note will receive a *secondary* accent.) In Example O "fun" and "__way" receive the chief accents, and "run" receives a secondary accent:

Example O

The bar line is badly placed in the following example; by chanting and playing it, you will see what I mean.

Example P

One way to begin setting words to music is to place bar lines before the accented syllables in important words, without regard to meter:

Example Q

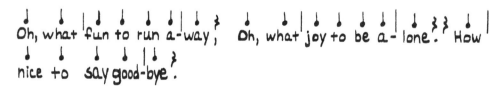

After finding the bar line, see if you can use a regular meter—either 3/4 or 4/4. If we add rests at the end of the first and second lines of Example Q, it falls nicely into 4/4:

Example R

In Example Q the words "Oh" and "what" are clearly preparatory, so the first *full* measure is labeled measure 1.

If we combine our use of ¼ notes and ½ notes with the intelligent use of bar line and meter, we might come up with the following (based on the same words that we have used for several examples now):

150

Example S

For several reasons, however, the solution in Example S is unsatisfactory. First, it does not express the comma at the end of line 1: line 1 runs into line 2 and the sense of separation between the two lines is lost. (The comma after "Oh" in both lines 1 and 2 indicates no separation; it is merely decorative.) It is also unsatisfactory with respect to the *number* of measures per line—lines 1 and 2 are three-measure lengths; what you must strive for in basic songwriting is *even measure length*—lines of two, four, six, or eight measures.

In Example T the ¼-note rests in measures 3, 4, 7, and 8 express the punctuation at the end of the first two lines. The addition of these rests results in four-measure units for lines 1 and 2 (line 3 is incomplete).

Example T

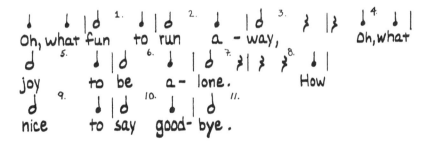

Exercise 7

1. Set the following words as chant (no pitches).

> His bags are packed, his way is clear.
> My son will leave this town.
> Once more a parent takes a stand.
> Once more a youth is ruled.

2. Write in 4/4 or 3/4 using ¼ notes and ½ notes, as well as ¼-note rests and ½-note rests.

3. Write the words before you write the rhythms—leave plenty of room for each syllable.

DOWNBEAT AND UPBEAT

Another consideration when setting words to be sung is successive ⅛ notes in 4/4 or 3/4 (time signatures in which the lower numeral is 4). The first of two successive ⅛ notes is like a ¼ note in accent and weight. The second note, the *upbeat*, is extremely weak, and is best used for unaccented syllables:

Example U

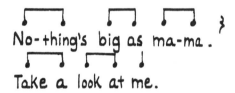

To use accented syllables on the upbeat and unaccented syllables on the downbeat, such as those shown in Example V, is courting disaster.

Example V

No-thing's big as ma-ma.
Take a look at me.

Exercise 8

Set these words as chant. Use mostly ⅛ notes, with some ¼ notes and ¼-note rests:

Oh, what fun to run a-way,

Oh, what joy to be a-lone.

COMBINATION OF THE ABOVE FACTORS
AND SOME CURIOUS CONSEQUENCES

These are the factors that we worked with, one by one, which you must deal with when you set words to music:

1. The bar line
2. Meter
3. Duration
4. Pitch
5. Downbeat versus upbeat
6. The rest
7. The number of measures in a phrase

When these factors are combined they modify each other. The word "run" in Example W is important: it is placed after the bar line and is given a longer duration. But note that it is also given the *lower* of the two pitches. In other words, an accented syllable of an important word does not have to be verified by *all* the factors at once, which I attempt to demonstrate in the following examples. Please sing all these examples.

Example W

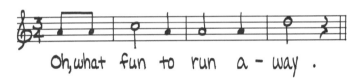

In Example X a rest is used after "fun," even though there is no punctuation. This use of a rest serves to emphasize the word preceding it.

Example X

In the simple syncopated pattern shown in Example Y, it is possible to set two accented syllables on the first two notes (as in *a*) or even to set an unaccented syllable right after the bar line (as in *b*):

Example Y

When the second of two ⅛ notes is a *high* tone, it is sometimes possible to give it an *accented* syllable:

Example Z

In Example AA note that the unaccented syllables are given to the high tones. This is acceptable because these are upbeats.

Example AA

In Example BB the ¼-note rest emphasizes the word "stop" by stopping at the rest.

Example BB

Another way to accent an important word is to use a *lower* pitch, which is especially effective when it is preceded by a skip, as in Example CC. (Note that the lower pitch has a ½-note duration and that it is preceded by the bar line).

Example CC

Exercise 9

1. Set the following text to music. Use any combination of the suggestions discussed in Examples W through CC, to make the meaning clear.

2. Use only tones of the C major scale.

3. Refer to the General Rules that are applicable, here and in all exercises.

You! All you do is spend my money,
Won't you ever be my honey?
Do, do, do!

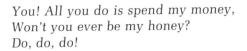

WORDS AND THE SMALL THEME

Now we are ready to turn to the small theme—the A (see Chapter 4). For this purpose, let us use the pentatonic scale, which we have used starting on the tone E. For songwriting, however, it is better to arrange the tones differently, starting on the tone G:

Example DD

But this scale would better suit our purposes built on the tone C, since it can then be harmonized in the key of C major, using the Basic Rules for Diatonic Progressions or the Basic Rules for Mixed Progressions:

Example EE

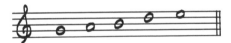

The lyric in Example FF is suitable for a small-theme procedure. All of the lines have the same number of syllables, and the first three lines have the same rhythm:

Example FF

Lord, what a day.
Look at the sun.
Blood in its eye.
Too hot to run.

From the rhythm of the words, we could construct a small theme of *a a a b*, *a b a c*, or *a a b c*. Since lines 1 and 2 are closest in meaning and rhythm and line 3 is quite different in meaning from the first two lines, the best form is *a a b c*:

Example GG

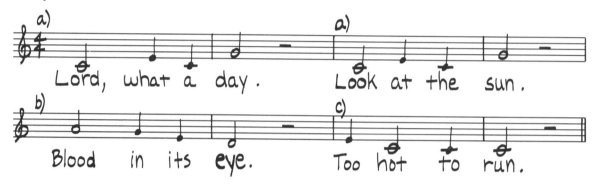

Notice the syncopation in measure 7, which gives an accent to both "too" and "hot." Also note that the *c* section uses lower tones than *b*, which allows the eight measures to be rounded off nicely.

Exercise 10

Harmony and accompaniment can improve a melody and can also affect the meaning of a text in different ways.

1. Harmonize the melody in Example GG according to the Basic Rules for Mixed Progressions. Be sure that the harmony is compatible with the text.
2. Use alphabetical chord symbols and place them above the staff precisely at the point in the measure where they are to take effect.
3. Use no more than two chords per measure. (Remember that all tones must be chord tones.)
4. Start and end with a C major triad.

In the *aa* of Example GG the words of the two lines are parallel: they have the same rhythms, and the important words fall in the same places. In Example HH below, the two lines have the same rhythm, but the important words fall in different places. (I have put arrows over the important words.)

Example HH

I have mét my love in dreáms,
He has held me clóse in dreáms,

156

In order to write identical melodies for these two lines, you must work very hard at finding a melody that will fit each line equally well. One approach is to emphasize "Dreams" and slightly suppress both "met" in line 1 and "close" in line 2:

Example II

Another approach is to treat "met my love" in line 1 and "held me close" in line 2 as *word groupings,* and then to put the emphasis on the word grouping:

Example JJ

Exercise 11

1. Compose an *a* that fits each of these lines equally well:

    Sweet Jane was quite a gal,
    She made the men feel good,

2. Use only the tones of the C pentatonic scale.

3. Use ½ notes, ¼ notes, and ⅛ notes and ½-note and ¼-note rests.

4. Do not exceed the range of an octave.

5. Of course you must be able to sing it!

Hint: Listen to the words carefully and see if they will amost set themselves. Use your intuition.

WORDS AND THE "AA"

Now we turn to composing the same melody for two matching stanzas. In the lyric in Example KK lines 1 and 5 have the same number of syllables and the same accents, as do lines 2 and 6, 3 and 7, and 4 and 8.

Example KK

1. *Sweet Jane was quite a gal,*
2. *And she knew it, too.*
3. *She made the men feel good,*
4. *Oh, what she could do.*

5. *She was a femme fatale,*
6. *And she knew it, too.*
7. *She made the women cry,*
8. *Oh, what she could do.*

In addition, *within* each stanza, the first and third lines correspond, as do the second and fourth lines. In Example LL I treat lines 1, 3, 5, and 7 as *a*; lines 2 and 6 as *b*; and lines 4 and 8 as *c*:

Example LL

Exercise 12

1. Compose an AA to these two stanzas after saying them aloud several times:

   I can speak to other men without a second thought,
   Sharing blue confessions with names I never caught.
   But when you walk my way the words start floating out of reach,
   I want to learn to turn my heartbeats into speech.

   I have burned up hours dreaming things you never say.
   Painting kind expressions 'til facts get in the way.
   Why can't I seem to put in words what just one touch would teach?
   I want to learn to turn my heartbeats into speech.

2. Use tones of the C major scale only.

3. Use ½ notes, ¼ notes, and ⅛ notes, and ½-note and ¼-note rests.

4. Harmonize what you have written with the diatonic major and minor triads of C major, beginning both A sections with C and ending the second A section with C (the first A section may end on an F or G chord).

Hint: Write *both* sets of words beneath the staff and then find tones that fit both sets of words equally well.

MORE ABOUT SINGABILITY

In the previous pages, I have touched on singability in the literal sense—what is easy to sing. Here are a few more suggestions on this topic:

1. Long notes are best sung on a vowel without an ending consonant, as in the words "go," "pray," or in the second syllable of the word "mama." There are two reasons for this: first, if the word ends with a consonant, the listener doesn't get its meaning until the word is concluded. Second, singers often ignore ending consonants, which they regard as an interruption to the flow of the vowel sound or because they don't know how to sing them properly. For either of these reasons, the meaning of the word is kept from the listener, and the point of music with words is the word.

2. High notes are also best on a vowel without an ending consonant.

3. But there are two vowels that are hard to sing high, especially loudly: *i* (as in "sift") and *e* (as in "free").

4. It is easier to sing high tones when they are approached gradually; this admonition underlies the physical basis for the *curve* in all melody, vocal and otherwise.

5. Beware of repeated tones, especially several tones of short note value, which tend to sound too much like ordinary speech:

Example MM

6. Long, sustained notes also reduce the intelligibility of the words; by the time you get to the last word you hardly know what it refers to:

Example NN

I sometimes think of the type of song that has been discussed in this chapter as *ordinary song*. Ordinary song reflects the words both in their meaning and in their rhythms: The words are understandable as sung and they derive from speech rhythms. Sometimes the same syllable will be of greater duration when used in ordinary song than when used in speech, but the general emphasis will be the same. Another characteristic of ordinary song is that the phrase lengths are regular—all four-measure or all eight-measure lengths, for example.

Strive to compose ordinary song in its most beautiful form. Strive for melodies that are shaped and memorable—that stick to the ears. Above all, strive for an elevated blending of words and music in which the two become one.

160

TWO INVALUABLE EXERCISES

Exercise 13

1. Find the sheet music for a standard popular song with an AABA structure by one of the song masters of the thirties or forties (Gershwin or Rodgers, for example). You should not be familiar with the song.

2. Study the way the words and music have been matched and write a paraphrase of the music line; in other words, compose your own melody but stress the words and syllables that the original composer stressed and follow the same AABA structure. (It is not important whether the words came first or the music came first in the original song.)

3. Base your melody on one of the scales used in this book.

4. Harmonize your setting according to the Basic Rules for Mixed Progressions. (You may use any of the non-chord tones we have discussed in this book.)

5. Study your versions and the original version carefully, both melodically and harmonically:

   a. Have the words and phrases been made clear or obscure?

   b. Do the two versions peak at the same point?

   c. Is the character of the lyric reflected in both settings?

   d. How have rhymes been handled in the music of the two versions?

   e. Is the music compatible with the lyrics of *all* the A's?

Exercise 14

1. Locate the lyric of a standard popular song written by one of the lyric masters of the thirties or forties (one by Ira Gershwin, Frank Loesser, or Lorenz Hart, for example). As in Exercise 13, the lyric should be from a song that is not familiar to you, and it should have an AABA structure. You must also find the sheet music for this song.

2. Do not look at the music before you set the words. Get the lyric from a lyric collection (the Ira Gershwin book listed in the Bibliography has several lyrics) or have someone dictate it to you. (In the latter case, make sure the person who dictates is able to distinguish between the intro, the A's, and the B.)

3. Set the lyric, following the principles outlined in this chapter. Speak the words out loud to find the natural rhythm. Note the important syllables, words, and phrases, and reflect these in your setting.

4. Parallel the AABA structure of the words in the melody and harmony (see Chapter 4). Determine the emotional curve of the lyric. As in music, a lyric will often peak near the end of the B.

5. Base your melody on one of the scales used in this book.

6. Harmonize your setting according to the Basic Rules for Mixed Progressions. (You may use any of the non-chord tones we have discussed in this book.)

7. *After* you have set the lyric, carefully compare your version with the original.

Hint: In some lyrics, a line or two may seem to have been added at the end of the song. This may be matched in the melody by a few related free measures that act as a *tag* to close off the song.

Exercise 14 is an extremely helpful one and periodically I do it myself.

AFTERTHOUGHTS

The main problem in writing ordinary song is finding the right text.

1. Try to find words that fit the characteristics of sung words in the left hand column of the list on pp. 144–45.

2. Look for stanzas that have repeated rhythms and meter. This gives you the possibility for repetition of small themes, especially of AA, which leads to AABA, the principal song form.

3. If you can't find such stanzaic correspondence, you can always repeat both *the words and the melody* of an A, thus achieving AA (see Schubert).

4. Make the B and the A contrasting in tone and mood (see Chapter 4), and, as I said before, let the B *sail back* into the A.

5. Find a poet or lyricist to whom you can explain some of the ideals of words for music.

Words humanize music. They keep music from becoming intellectual and remote. They keep music in touch with an audience. Remember that music with words allows you to tell a story—to express a specific idea or emotion in addition to what the music alone is expressing. Music alone can of course be very expressive, but lyrics and music together can reach a level of expressivity rarely found in any other art form.

14

Picture Music

Picture music includes all music that is written without actual tones (see Example A). Sometimes this type of music looks more like a drawing than a piece of music, as you will see later in this chapter.

Composing picture music is like playing tennis without the net; there are no rules, only procedures. Your intention is expressed in broad strokes because you cannot be as precise as in conventional notation.

I believe in rules and in guidelines; this workbook is filled with them. Rules and guidelines help you to focus your creative energy by defining the task. You will find this to be true even later, when you have graduated from the rudimentary procedures outlined here.

In place of rules, picture music offers something else: you will begin to rethink the entire process of music. You will get a new perspective through the *visualization* that picture music offers, and thus your conventional music making will be improved.

It must be admitted that picture music is inadequately notated, but I should like to point out that conventional notation is very limited itself and owes more to the performance than is generally realized; a good piece often sounds entirely unlike what the composer had in mind.

Example A is for *found* instruments: key chain, wastepaper basket, and rubber band. Get together with two other people and "perform" this example. Be sure to study the characteristics of each "instrument." Take this seriously and you will be amply repaid. (All the exercises and examples in this chapter should be performed, when possible.)

Example A

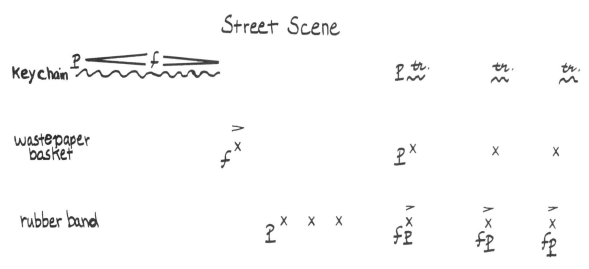

Exercise 1

To make picture music, you need picture equipment: several different-color felt-tip markers ("Marko" by Flair is very good, as I noted earlier) and art paper (from 15 inches by 18 inches to eighteen inches by twenty inches).

1. Write a short piece for three found instruments. Look hard for good ones and investigate the sound possibilities of each.
2. Write lengthwise on the paper. When you reach the right-hand margin, go to a second sheet of paper. This will give you a better idea of the piece than trying to write the whole piece on one sheet.
3. This piece should be from thirty to sixty seconds in length.
4. Specify the tempo in a general way (we are not using a regular pulse or beat here, but the order of events from left to right can move quickly or slowly).
5. *Line up the three parts* so that events that occur simultaneously are exactly lined up vertically.
6. Use a different-color marker for each instrument and black ink for all indications (dynamics, name of instrument, and so on). The players will do a better job for you if the part looks like you invested some time in it.

7. Express some idea or mood and stick to it. Use a title that captures this idea or mood. Perhaps you will want to make these works portraits of someone you know or of a historical figure.

8. Have the players enter at different times so that each part will stand out.

9. Refer to the General Rules that are applicable (pages 1 to 3), especially with reference to titles.

THE HUMAN VOICE

Now let us turn to the voice. Musical pitch (up and down) is expressed by a curved line: In Example B, *a* could be interpreted in actual notes as at *b*:

Example B

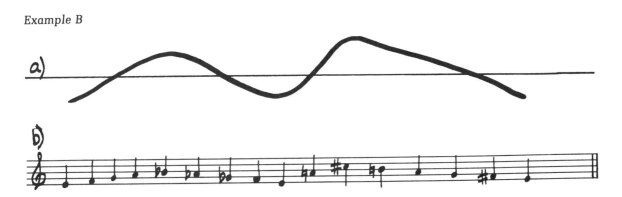

The higher the line is on the paper the higher it is in pitch, and, conversely, the lower the line the lower the pitch. Try to preserve distinctions: if the line goes a *little* lower at one point than another, the tone you sing should be a little lower too. For this reason, I recommend the use of a *guide line*—the horizontal straight line in Example B above. The guide line should be black.

An ascending or descending *straight* line at an angle indicates a glissando:

Example C

To indicate a rest (perhaps for breath), leave spaces in the line.

Example D

Short notes are indicated by dots and longer notes by dashes (the length of which may vary):

Example E

Show connected long notes thus:

Example F

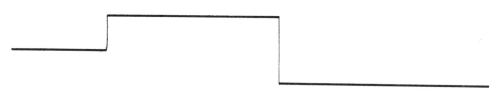

In addition to words, which we will get to soon, a large variety of vocal sounds is available. Here are only a few:

Example G

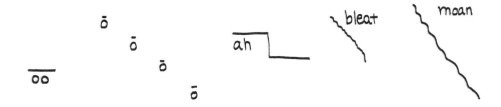

Notes can also be altered in many ways. Example H shows some of them: *a)* a bend, *b)* a "fall-off," *c)* a "fall-up," *d)* a "doink," and *e)* a trill (short and long):

Example H

Exercise 2

1. Write a short piece for solo voice (female or male) of forty to sixty seconds in duration.

2. Use as many of the resources shown in Examples B through H as you can.

3. Use pen, marker, and art paper, as in Exercise 1.

TWO VOICES

In Example I, I have written for *two* voices. Note the two vertical lines (which should be black, like the guide line) that serve to show the performers the coinciding points for the two voices and also give either a general idea of duration or a specific duration, as shown here. Pieces for more than one player may be "conducted" (that is, the vertical lines may be designated by a conductor) or self-conducted. In either case, everybody will have to pay close attention to everybody else to see how each part is progressing. When timings are used, a large sweep second clock is necessary if the pieces are to be self-conducted.

Example I

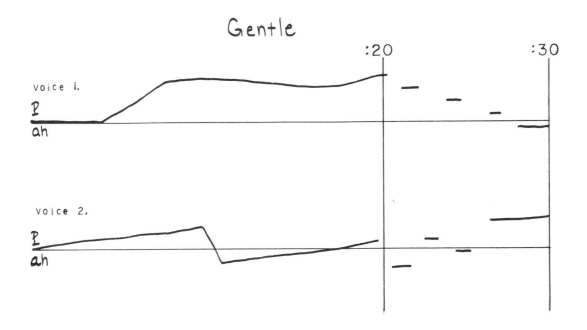

In Example J, I have been more ambitious:

Example J

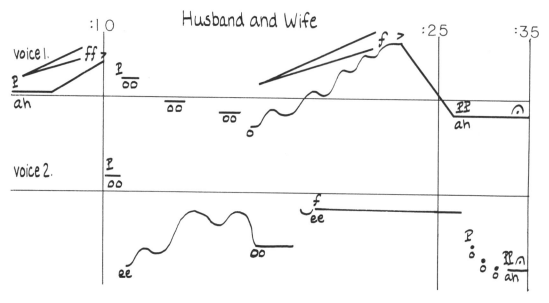

Exercise 3

1. Write a short piece for two voices lasting no less than thirty seconds.

2. Use any of the resources thus far shown.

3. Use a different color marker for each voice and write on art paper. Be sure to use occasional black vertical lines to help the performers line up their parts. Give timings too.

THE VOICE AND WORDS

The use of words is the special and greatest resource of the voice because words express concrete ideas and feelings. Let us begin with *spoken* words, which are indicated with an x:

Example K

This type of passage also works well if two or more people perform it, in which case you will sometimes want to use actual rhythms (but not necessarily bar lines or meter):

Example L

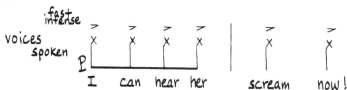

168

The *shout* is also useful on occasion. (Perform this example first with one person and then with two or more.)

Example M

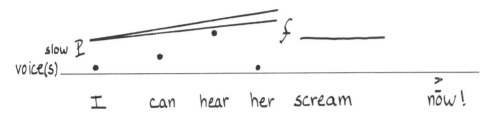

Use x's only for spoken or shouted words. For *sung* words, proceed as follows:

Example N

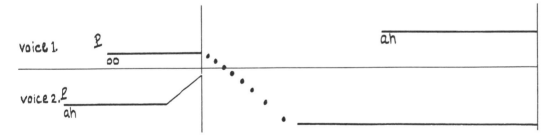

Try the preceding example with two or more voices, also. Start on two different pitches, to get different parts.

When you use markers of different colors, you can clearly indicate *crossing* (the upper voice beneath the lower voice for a short time), a delightful technique. Imagine how much clearer the following example would be if the first voice were written in red and the second in blue:

Example O

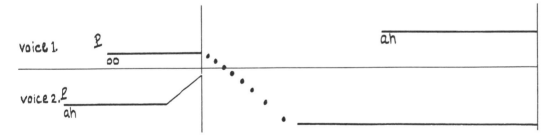

Exercise 4

1. Write a piece for male or female voices (specify which) of more than a minute in length.
2. Use the following words in any way you want (repeat them, use an important word by itself, and so forth):

> *Rain will kiss the baby's brow.*
> *Rain, now.*

3. Remember that you don't have to use all voices at once all the time. If you write for three voices, for example, you have three solos, two different duos, and so forth. Be economical: remember that *less is more.*

4. Write on art paper and use any of the resources discussed in this chapter. Stretch yourself and open your ear.

WIND AND STRING INSTRUMENTS

Much of what I have discussed here is applicable to wind and string instruments. In Example P I have taken advantage of the flute's great facility:

Example P

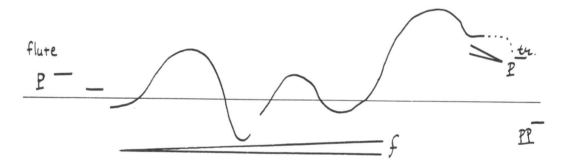

And here is a *duo*—a duet for flute and oboe:

Example Q

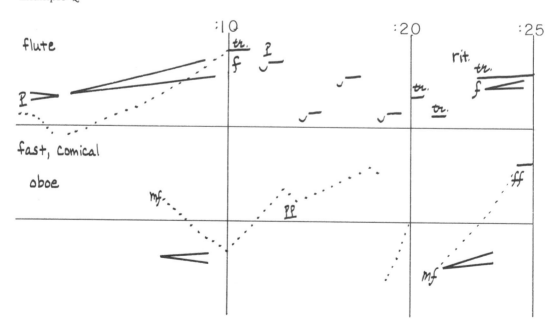

Exercise 5

1. Write a short piece (one or two minutes long) for two wind instruments, preferably in different ranges, such as flute and bassoon.

2. Use art paper and markers.

3. Employ all resources that are set forth in this chapter and utilize your knowledge of the special qualities of the instruments you are writing for.

In Example R, which is for violin and cello, I have made use of some special characteristics of string instruments—pizzicato and slap pizzicato:

Example R

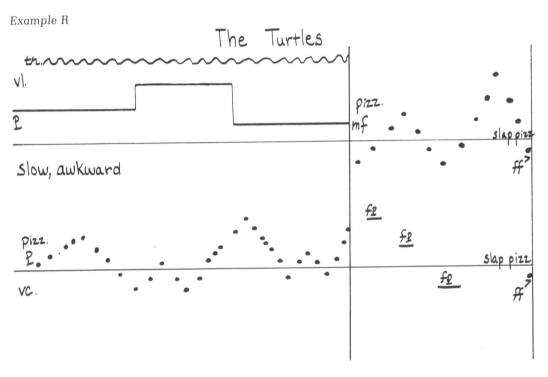

In addition to the special characteristics of instruments, you should become familiar with their unusual, extravagant characteristics, such as the sound made by woodwinds when they are fingered but not blown through. Such a resource is shown in Example S;

Example S

When you write in sync for two or more instruments, it is wise to use actual rhythms, as shown below:

Example T

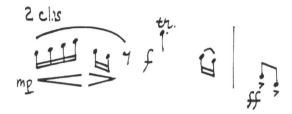

THE CANON

A *canon* consists of two or more voices, identical to each other but starting at different points. ("Three Blind Mice" is a form of canon.) Canons work well with the resources we are discussing in this chapter, and I will show you what one looks like:

Example U

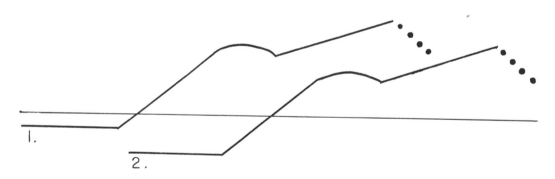

Exercise 6

1. Write a canon for two instruments, as in Example U.
2. Write it out in full and use a different color for each instrument.

VERBAL MUSIC

Another form of picture music is *verbal* music:

172

Example V

Battle

tpt.
solo
short
notes f
fan bell
with plgr.
long washs p
long
notes mf
1 tone
many
times mf
p o

tb.
long
notes
sm. gliss mf
solo
high,
erratic f
long
notes mf ⟶
p o

db.
pizz.
long
notes
(vibr.) p
long
notes mf
harmonics
only
solo mf
p o

Example W shows verbal music combined with the more basic picture-music resources. In addition, it employs *boxes*, which help the performance. The Roman numeral IV tells the string players to use their fourth string (the lowest string) where indicated.

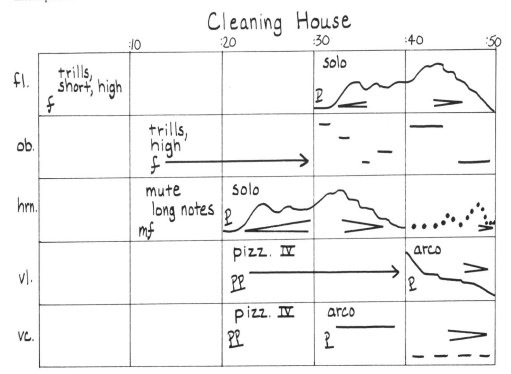

Cleaning House

Exercise 7

1. Write an example of verbal music using either of the two methods discussed.
2. Use three to five instruments.
3. The duration should be not less than two minutes.

KEYBOARD INSTRUMENTS

When writing for a keyboard instrument, you might want to use *clusters*, which are bunches of keys hit with either or both hands or forearms. The process in Example X differentiates between black-note clusters (*a*) and white-note clusters (*b*). At *c* I have shown a method of indicating clusters of mixed black and white notes. I have used treble and bass clefs here, but feel free to use only a guide line if you wish. The duration of the cluster is indicated by the *width* of the box.

Example X

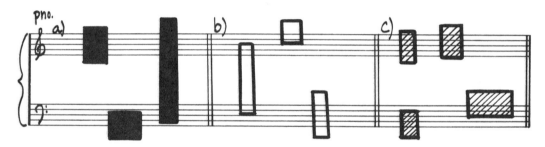

Exercise 8

1. Write a piece for piano thirty to sixty seconds long.
2. Use clusters and chords as in Example X, as well as other resources of picture music. Two hands permit two parts.
3. Use a guide line or two staffs, as desired.

MORE ON THE CURVE

By this time it should be clear to you that picture music will help you to compose conventional music, that picture music is a visualization of conventional music, and that good pictures lead to good pieces. As an example of this, let us return to the subject of the curve, which I discussed in an earlier chapter.

In either picture music or conventional music, avoid melodic curves that simply go up and down:

Example Y

or that go up and down several times the same way:

Example Z

Strive for a series of curves:

Example AA

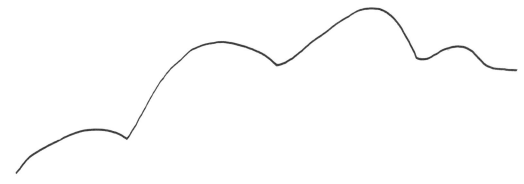

Generally, avoid sudden leaps up:

Example BB

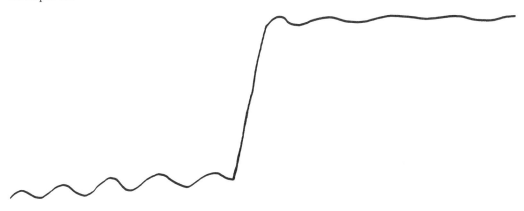

A melody that goes straight down is likely to be weak:

Example CC

When writing two or more simultaneous melodies, make sure that they do not have identical curves (except for organum, of course!):

Example DD

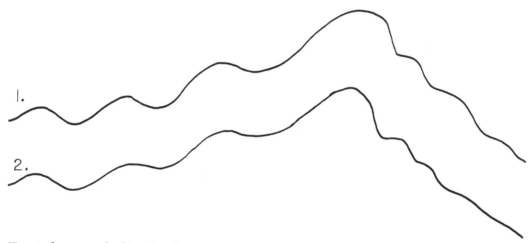

Try to have melodies that have *different* shapes—that reach their peaks at different points:

Example EE

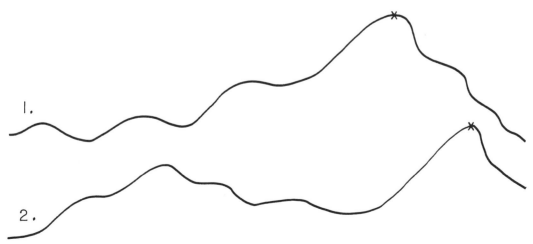

176

PERCUSSION INSTRUMENTS

In addition to wind and string instruments and piano, percussion instruments can also be used in a picture piece. Either by themselves or with the other instruments, they offer an enormous number of resources.

Exercise 9

1. Write a picture piece for one percussion instrument and two other instruments, either winds or strings.
2. Use all the procedures listed in this chapter.
3. The piece should be at least two minutes long but not longer than three minutes. Strive for mood and tone.
4. Specify dynamics and other performance instructions, *copiously*.

15

Popular Music as a Source

Popular music has invigorated art music through the centuries. All composers of art music have drawn on popular music as a source. "Art music" is the best phrase I can think of to describe music in which humanitarian aims coincide with well developed craft. Sometimes this is called "serious music"—a term that I dislike because it suggests a disapproval of popular music.

Popular music has helped to keep composers in touch with their audience—that is, until the mid-twentieth century, when composers turned away from their audiences (and from popular music), with disastrous results. As the tone of this book suggests, I am concerned with maintaining *good relations* with the audience; I see the composer as a moral force, as an instructor, and as an essential contributor to the good life. So it should come as no surprise that much of this book points toward beauty and simplicity and that we now turn to popular music as a source for art music.

ART MUSIC WITH POPULAR ELEMENTS: SCALES

One way to use popular music as a source is to draw on it in part, to use elements of it. For example, popular music through the ages makes abundant use of the pentatonic scale, especially the forms built on E and G:

Example A

In Example B, I use the E form of the pentatonic scale to construct a folk-like melody.

Example B

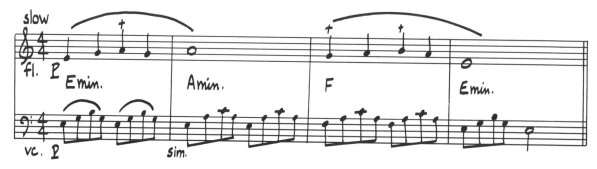

The G form of the pentatonic scale is also very rich in source material. Let us transpose it to C, as we did in Chapter 13.

Example C

This is the scale that Dvořák used in his famous symphony *From the New World*. The transposed form allows us to use C major harmonizations, as in Example D:

Example D

Exercise 1

1. Compose a small theme of folk-like quality using only the tones of the C pentatonic scale.

2. Here, as elsewhere, you may wish to evolve chords for your melody and then to construct an accompaniment of some sort. Restrict your attempts at harmony to the material covered in this book; this material is very limited, but it will keep you out of trouble and it will prepare you for more advanced work.

3. Refer to the General Rules that are applicable, here and in all exercises.

180

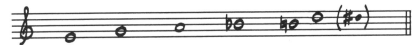

The blues scale also offers great opportunities. I have written it out in Example E, adding D♯, which is usually used as a non-chord tone:

Example E

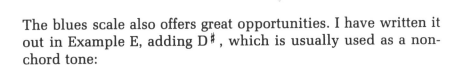

Using the tones in the scale in Example E, I constructed four major and minor triads:

Example F

Example G is based on this blues scale and draws on the major and minor triads that can be evolved from it. Note the use of neighboring tones on strong beats that resolve up a minor 2nd; this use of neighboring tones is quite distinctive and is employed relentlessly, which serves to unify the passage:

Example G

Exercise 2

1. Compose a small theme to the given chords, using only the tones of the expanded blues scale (see Example E), either as chord tones or as non-chord tones (treat non-chord tones with great care; use your ear).

2. Use only two or three rhythms.

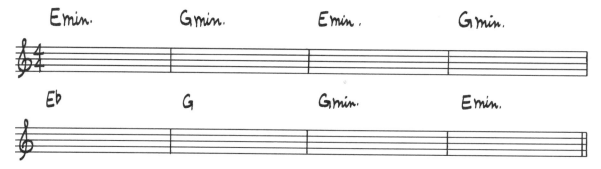

The blues scale is used again in Example H. Here the melody and the chords hardly seem to fit together, since so many tones in the melody are non-chord tones. However some of these non-chord tones are *blue notes*—the minor 3rd and minor 7th of a major triad; because of blues and jazz, the ear perceives these as almost legitimate chord tones when used in a blues or jazz style, as is the case here.

Example H

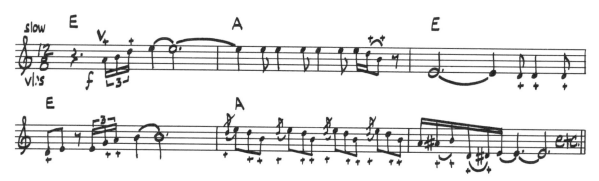

Exercise 3

1. Compose a blues-like melody using the tones of the expanded blues scale. The given chords are the traditional chords of the blues, but you may write "around" them as I did in Example H, with the melody and chords coming together only at points.

2. Irregularity of rhythms is all right here, but confine yourself to the Basic Note Values. You may treat successive ⅛ notes as "*inégales*" (see Chapter 4).

Example I shows a characteristic blues phrase, the tones of which
I then lay out in scale form:

Example I

Using the tones in Example I as a cell, I evolved the following
four passages. Although these passages are not in a blues style,
the force of the cell is so strong that a blues quality comes
through. (This material is taken from "*Street Music, A Blues Con-
certo,*"* in which I used this cell extensively):

Example J

Exercise 4

Compose a small theme using only the tones given in Example I.
Start and end on C.

ART MUSIC WITH
POPULAR ELEMENTS: RHYTHM

So far we have been looking at some non-pop ways of using
essential characteristics or elements of popular *melody*. Here are
some ways of using popular *rhythms* in a piece.

The following rhythm is from Scott Joplin's ragtime piece "The
Entertainer":

Example K

Here is the same rhythm with a new melody (based on the tones
of the C ditonic scale):

Example L

Here are the first few measures of "Turkey in the Straw":

Example M

Here is a paraphrase of this melody, with the same rhythm and
new tones, which are drawn from the blues cell seen in Example
I:

Example N

The rhythm that follows is a characteristic jazz rhythm:

Example O

Using the rhythm in Example O combined with the tones of the
C Lixian scale, I have constructed this melody:

Example P

Exercise 5

1. Use the rhythm of "The Entertainer" in Example K and find
   new tones that are appropriate to it.

2. Draw these tones from a procedure in this book: the cell, the row, or a particular scale, for instance. Write your source above the piece and *label* the procedure.

Exercise 6

Follow the rules for Exercise 5, but here use the rhythm of "Turkey in the Straw."

Exercise 7

Again, complete this exercise as you did Exercise 5 and 6, this time using the given rhythms and the tones of the Scriabin chord: C F♯ B♭ E A D.

ART MUSIC WITH
POPULAR ELEMENTS: MELODY

Earlier we looked at the use of melodic characteristics such as blue notes, the pentatonic scale, and the blues scale. Other sources that popular music offers are the melodies themselves. (Here it is better to restrict yourself to public-domain songs, which are not covered by copyright and may be used freely.) Let us take "I'm a Wayfarin' Stranger," a well known folk song. Here are the first eight measures:

186

Example Q

In Example R we see this same succession of tones, the durations of which have been altered by irregular diminution and augmentation. Note that the melody, which is in D Dorian, has been harmonized with chords from D Dorian. Also note the reverse neighboring tones in measures 4 and 8 and the long neighboring tone in measure 9; such uses work best in simple, diatonic passages.

Example R

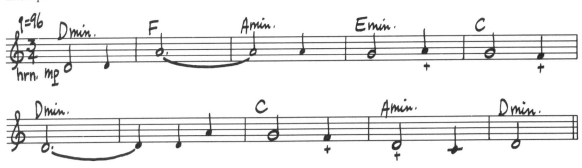

Exercise 8

Apply irregular augmentation and diminution to "I'm a Wayfarin' Stranger."

Exercise 9

Harmonize your version of "I'm a Wayfarin' Stranger," according to the Basic Rules for Diatonic Chord Progressions. Use alphabetical chord symbols and place them above the staff.

Irregular augmentation and diminution are employed again in Example S, as is reiteration (the circled tone). In addition, I have *inflected* five tones (with sharps):

Example S

Exercise 10

Apply any of the transformational procedures discussed in Chapter 3 to the melody of "I'm a Wayfarin' Stranger."

It must be clear by now that a song like "I'm a Wayfarin' Stranger" lends itself to countless procedures, whether you use the entire melody or only a portion of it, as we have here. If you use the *entire* melody, apply the theme and variations techniques, which are laid out in Chapter 3.

Some of you may fear that the procedures described in this chapter will lead to pieces that lack originality. Don't worry. If you have talent, it will emerge. Borrowing creatively is good for you—and good for music too. If it "sounds like I've heard it somewhere before," the chances are that you're getting the point.

ART MUSIC WITH
POPULAR ELEMENTS: ACCOMPANIMENT

In this section, we turn to popular sources for accompaniment, which popular music offers in abundance. The bass line in Example T is a good example. It is drawn from the blues; I found it irresistible to work with (it is used throughout the third movement of another blues work of mine, *Three Pieces for Blues Band and Orchestra*).* To this ostinato, I composed a melody for the violins. Note that all of the non-chord tones except the first can be thought of as members of the blues scale. (Transpose the blues scale from E down a major 2nd to make this clear; however, you should be able to *hear* it when it is played.)

Example T

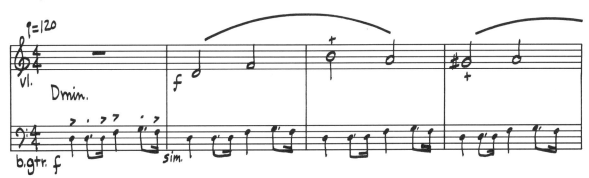

*Excerpts from *Three Pieces for Blues Band and Orchestra* Op. 50 by William Russo.
©Copyright 1973 by Southern Music Publishing Co., Inc.
©Copyright 1974 by Southern Music Publishing Co., Inc.
International copyright secured.
All rights reserved including the right of public performance for profit.
Used by permission.

Exercise 11

Using the expanded blues scale, write a non-pop small theme to
the ostinato accompaniment given.

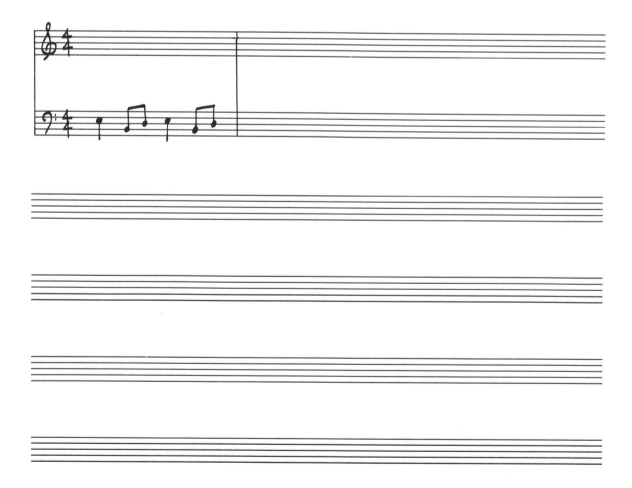

The following example consists of a bluegrass banjo figure written out in notes twice as long as in the original:

Example U

I have taken this figure, displaced it by an ⅛ note, and put it into 5/4. At a slow tempo, it is interesting enough to become the beginning of a melodic line. Notice that the chords are drawn from the melody.

Example V

ART MUSIC WITH
POPULAR ELEMENTS: PROCEDURE

So far we have talked about drawing from popular sources, sources from which we can depart. Here I will suggest something different: that we apply popular *procedures* to material that is non-pop.

One such procedure we have already discussed: changing successive ⅛ notes to uneven ⅛ notes "in the jazz manner" or *inégales*. Take a melody with successive ⅛ notes:

Example W

and change the successive ⅛ notes to dotted ⅛s, and ¹⁄₁₆s (uneven ⅛s):

Example X

Exercise 12

Apply uneven ⅛ notes to any non-pop example in this book that
has an abundance of successive ⅛ notes.

Another procedure is to assign a distinctly popular instrument
to a passage that is non-pop:

Example Y

Exercise 13

Designate another popular instrument that would suit Example
Y, above.

In the following passage I have applied a jazz procedure ("wah's," with plunger) to a "straight" melody:

Example Z

To *a*, following, I have applied jazz rhythms; the result is *b*.

Example AA

And *b*, following, is a "tango-ized" form of *a*:

Example BB

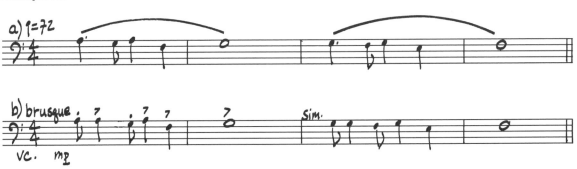

ADDING A POPULAR ACCOMPANIMENT

Earlier in the chapter I talked about writing a non-pop melody to a pop accompaniment. Here again you can reverse the process. In Example U the melody (in the bass) came first and the bluegrass-style accompaniment was added to it. Note the blue notes in the accompaniment:

Example CC

In Example DD I have added a rock-and-roll accompaniment to a lyrical melody. Note the consonant intervals between the two voices on the first beat of each measure. Try to hear each of the parts played separately and then together.

Example DD

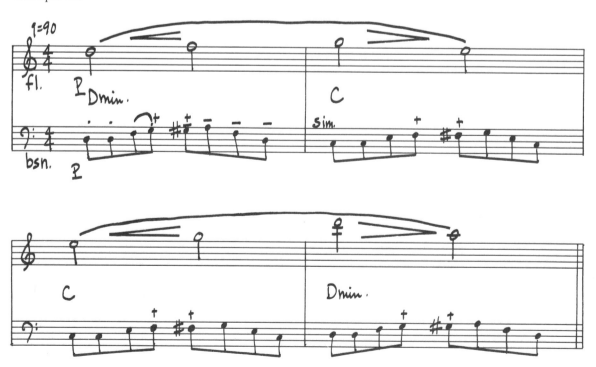

194

Exercise 14

Write an accompaniment to the given melody in one of two ways:

1. Compose a pop-type ostinato figure for a bass-clef instrument, moving the figure along with the chords. Find a figure that fits well throughout (not just for the first couple of measures).

2. Write a repeated-tone accompaniment of a pop nature for piano (all in the bass clef), such as:

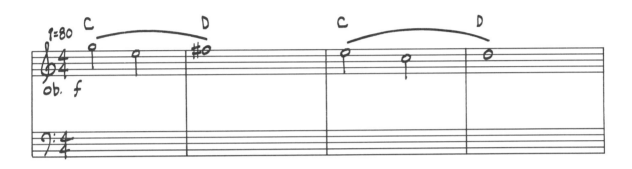

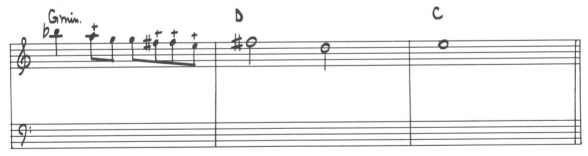

TWISTING POPULAR ACCOMPANIMENTS

Whether they are written before or after the melody, accompaniments drawn from popular styles can be "twisted." Take the

accompaniment figuration in Example EE, which is an ordinary
one-measure ostinato:

Example EE

Here is the same ostinato minus two ⅛ notes, which creates a
superimposition of 3/4 against the 4/4 meter.

Example FF

Here is another standard ostinato:

Example GG

Here is the ostinato from Example GG made into a seven-note
figuration that goes against the meter in the same way that Example FF does:

Example HH

Now here is the original ostinato (Example GG) completely
unchanged but in 3/4 instead of 4/4:

Example II

In *a* of Example JJ we have "oom-pah," in Tin Pan Alley style;
b is the same accompaniment stretched out into 5/4:

Example JJ

Exercise 15

"Twist" this accompaniment in two or three of the ways
described:

JUXTAPOSITION OF
ART MUSIC AND POPULAR MUSIC

So far I have discussed the *blending* of popular music and art
music. It was only recently, however, that I discovered how
easily music can move from one style to another—how two or
more styles can be *juxtaposed*. Part *a* of Example BB shows a
melodic theme that was the basis for the processional at a Columbia College commencement. This theme is severe and dignified—

very non-pop. We were just about through playing the piece when the stage manager signaled me that we had to fill in with ten minutes of music. I indicated to the pianist that he should improvise upon the theme; he did so, eloquently. Then a burst of inspiration hit me, and I asked the bass player to add a jazz bass line; the pianist moved into a jazz improvisation, and it worked wonderfully, continuing with several improvised solos by other instruments. As the last of the graduates moved to their seats, I brought the orchestra back into the processional as originally conceived (as a "serious" piece), and the juxtaposition between the pop and the non-pop was a complete success.

Since then I have worked with juxtaposition between non-pop and pop styles in many of my pieces, and I am happy to report that it is a procedure that holds a great deal of promise. To go much further in discussing this procedure would be beyond the intention of this book, but I want to plant the idea in your mind.

One last word: You must *always* believe in the popular music you draw on, or what you write will be self-conscious and false. These exercises will open you up to the immense possibilities that stylistic mixtures offer you, but you must be honest in using these possibilities.

16

Minimalism

ISORHYTHM REVISITED

Minimalism means using less to achieve more. Much of this book is based on minimalistic procedures: the cell, the row, and the use of Basic Note Values, for example. Minimalism also has stylistic and aesthetic implications, which I will discuss after developing minimalistic procedures further.

Exercise 1

This exercise is based on an isorhythm and pitch restrictions— two procedures that you know about already, although they are used slightly differently here:

1. The isorhythm given is four measures in length and uses tones from the C pentatonic scale.
2. Use this exact rhythm in the second four measures, the third four measures, and the fourth four measures. Be sure to restrict yourself to tones found in the C pentatonic scale: C D E G A.
3. End on the tone C.
4. Refer to the General Rules that are applicable, here and in all exercises.

BUILDING BLOCKS

Exercise 2

1. Note the one-measure subfigurations in the first four measures; they are derived from a cell: E G A B. These subfigurations are labeled *a*, *b*, *c*, and *d*. They should be thought of as *building blocks*.

2. I have indicated where these building blocks are to be used; you must fill in the measures with the correct building block.

   Hint: This is a simple way to use the subfiguration *transformational procedure* (see Chapter 3).

Exercise 3

1. Use the following building blocks *a*, *b*, *c*, and *d* in any order.

2. The last one or two measures may be free so that you can bring the piece to a close; use only the tones of the C pentatonic scale.

3. Harmonize the melody with alphabetical chord symbols derived from the Basic Rules for Diatonic Progressions.

4. In this case, since all tones are diatonic and the chords you use will be diatonic, you may treat the tone A in the first measure as a non-chord tone, even though it is a ½ note. Use your ear.

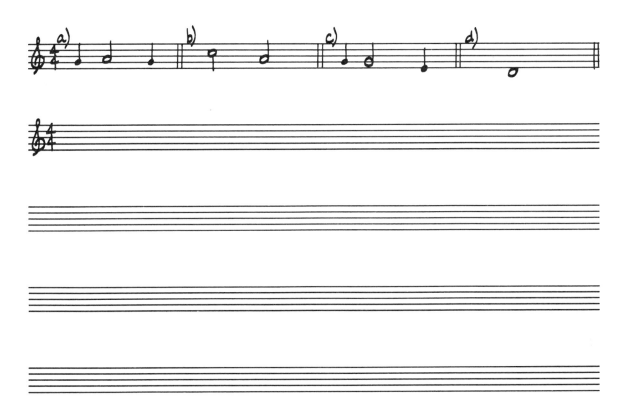

POINTILLISM

In Example A the melody has been divided among four instruments. Note that the horn and the trombone are muted, making them more similar in tone color and volume to the flute and clarinet. Also note that each of the parts is *playable*—that the parts do not contain awkward rhythms, such as two ⅛ notes followed by a rest. This procedure of dividing a melody between two or more instruments is called *pointillism*.

Example A

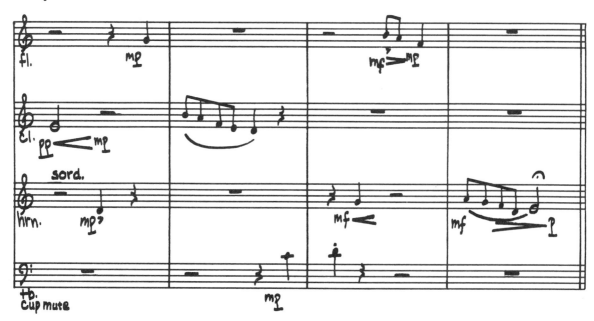

Exercise 4

Write out the melody of the preceding example on one staff.

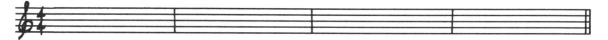

Exercise 5

1. Apply pointillism to a in the music shown; you may also change the octave of any tone whenever you wish (octave displacement is another characteristic of pointillism).

2. Use three instruments, which you must specify.

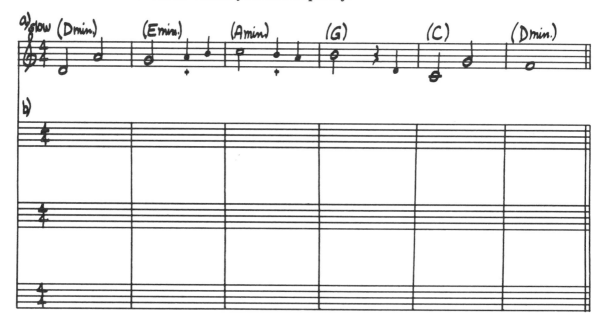

THE FALSE SECOND VOICE

In Example B I show a simple melody in D Dorian, harmonized with chords from D Dorian. (Note the double passing tones in measure two; these are acceptable because they are of short duration and because the harmony is diatonic.)

Example B

Example C shows the melody of Example B divided between two instruments pointillistically. However, there is one principal difference between this example and Example A: tones are held over, creating the illusion of two-part writing. This process can be applied only when the held-over tone belongs to the chord. It is not a good idea to hold a tone over when it is *above* the melody unless the instrument that is holding over is the weaker of the two instruments, as in measure 2. Also note in measure 3 that I have created a *false second voice* by adding a tone to the oboe part; such added tones must be *beneath* the true melody so that the true melody is not obscured. (The true melody is marked with vertical arrows.)

Example C

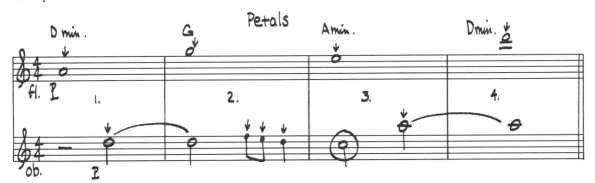

Exercise 6

1. Apply the process shown in Example C to the melody and chords (C Lixian) given.

2. Make sure that the stronger of the two instruments does not hold over a tone above the true melody. Hold tones over only when they are part of the harmony.

3. Create a false second voice if you can.

4. Refer to the General Rules that are applicable, here and in all exercises.

HETEROPHONY

Another form of minimalism is shown in Example D. It is called
heterophony, two forms of one melody played simultaneously.
In this example the lower part is the original melody and the
upper part is an embellishment of the original melody.

Example D

Exercise 7

1. The original melody is given in the bass clef.

2. In the treble clef, compose an embellished form of the original
   melody, using chord tones and non-chord tones (which need
   not correspond to the C Lixian scale if chosen with care). Use
   only Basic Note Values.

3. The embellished form must be in a different octave than the
   original melody and must stay out of the original melody's
   way: give each melody elbow room, as I have suggested
   before. Also, be sure that the two melodies sound good
   together. Use your ear, as always. (You do not have to be
   guided by the rules of counterpoint here. A little friction is
   appropriate to heterophony.)

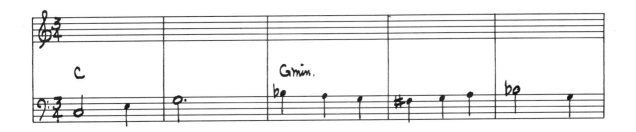

Another form of heterophony is shown below in Example E. It consists of the original melody (the upper part) and a *rhythmically* altered form of that melody (the lower part) played simultaneously. At *a*, the lower part is displaced—it is an ⅛ note late; at *b*, the lower part consists of an irregular augmentation and diminution of the upper part:

Example E

Exercise 8

Compose a rhythmically altered form of the given melody in the lower octave (you may use dotted ½ notes and ties here as well as the Basic Note Values):

MORE ON BUILDING BLOCKS

Exercise 9

1. The bass-clef accompaniment to the melody is to be filled in with the building blocks labeled *a)* and *b)*. These are like the building blocks in Exercise 2 in that they work well in almost any order. But note that they are used simultaneously as well as consecutively.

2. Fill in these building blocks as indicated. The last measure may be freely composed to round off the piece.

3. Refer to the General Rules that are applicable, here and in all exercises.

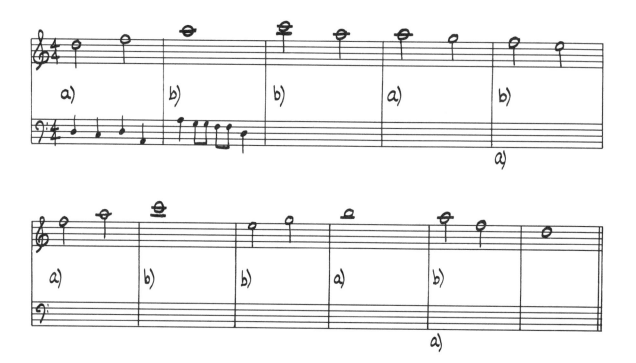

TWO OR MORE OSTINATOS AT ONCE

I would now like to develop the simultaneous use of more than one ostinato pattern (as employed in Exercise 9) a little further. The simultaneous ostinato accompaniment patterns seen in Example F, *a*, can be *transposed* down a major 2nd, as at *b*.

When constructing an entire piece of music, you might begin with a section ten to twenty measures long built on *a*. It could be followed by a ten-to-twenty-measure section built on *b*, using either the same theme for both sections (transposed down a major 2nd for part *b*, of course) or two different themes. Either way, you could return to the first section built on *a*, using the first theme or a new theme.

Hint: Note carefully that non-chord tones occur only in one part at a time. Also, since all tones in this example are from the pentatonic scale, in which there are only three slightly dissonant intervals (see Chapter 10), serious clashes are less likely.

Example F

Exercise 10

Write out *a* in Example F down a perfect 5th:

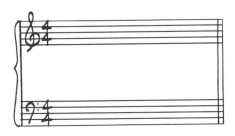

This type of accompaniment is so basic and so powerful that it will bear large-scale repetition. But you may wish to modify such large-scale repetition by means of transposition, as shown in Example F, or by a different process, as shown in Example G: here, each of the patterns is altered slightly, one at a time, and very gradually over a substantial number of measures. (A changed pattern is shown by an arrow.) This procedure will hold up for as long as five minutes, depending on how good the materials are and also on how deeply you wish to delve into the experience of Eastern "timelessness," from which this type of accompaniment is derived.

Example G

Veda

Exercise 11

Slightly alter each of the following ostinato patterns, one at a time, as in Example G. (Use arrows to show the change of patterns.)

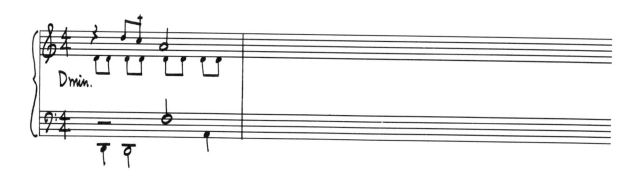

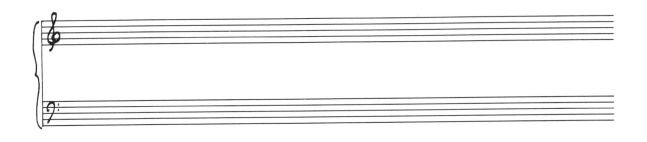

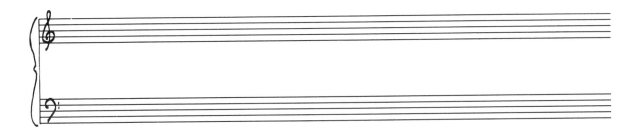

You can also "stack" the ostinato patterns *differently,* as shown in *b:*

Example H

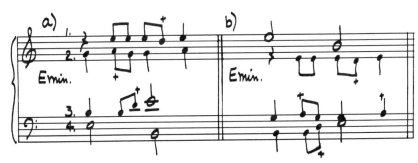

Exercise 12

1. Number the ostinato patterns in Example H, *b.*
2. Stack the patterns of Example H, *a* in yet another way.

KALEIDOSCOPIC OSTINATOS

An excellent minimalistic accompaniment procedure is to compose two simultaneous ostinatos, each with a different number of beats (not divisible into each other), as shown in Example I, where the relationship between the two patterns keeps changing until they come back together in measure 4. Compare this to out-of-sync isomelody and isorhythm, which takes place within one voice (see Chapter 6):

Example I

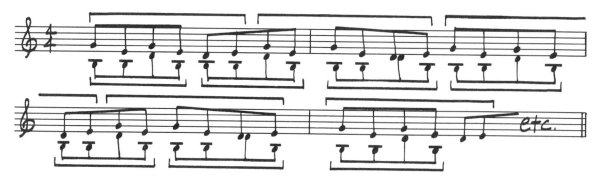

Exercise 13

1. Compose two ostinatos, using the tones of the D minor triad and neighboring tones, to these rhythms:

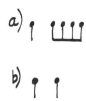

2. Write them out in full for the three measures it takes before they coincide again. (It is especially important to hear how these two patterns sound in relationship to each other.)

I refer to this procedure as *kaleidoscopic*: two or more ostinatos of unequal length out of sync with each other. Example J is based on the E pentatonic scale (E G A B D), and it consists of four ostinato patterns: *a* is twelve beats long, *b* is three beats long, *c* is one and a half beats long, and *d* is two beats long. These four patterns come together every three measures.

Example J

Exercise 14

1. In the two lower staffs of each system given, compose a new kaleidoscope accompaniment based on the rhythms of Example J; use only tones of the E pentatonic scale.

2. If possible, play *a* and *b*, *a* and *c*, *a* and *d*, and so on, at the piano to make sure each pair of patterns works together for the full three measures.

Exercise 15

1. Compose a melody on the upper staff for the accompaniment you wrote in Exercise 14. Again, use only tones of the E pentatonic scale. (For the melody to stand out, it should probably be written higher than the accompaniment.)

2. Use only this rhythm:

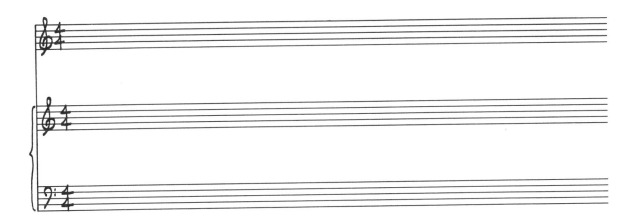

A more extensive use of the kaleidoscope principle is seen in Example K, in which the patterns come together after fifteen measures: *a* is four beats long, *b* is three beats long, *c* is five beats long, and *d* is six beats long. In this example I have based all of the patterns on tones from the E minor 7th chord (three stacked thirds), which you can also think of as E G B D from the E pentatonic scale.

Example K

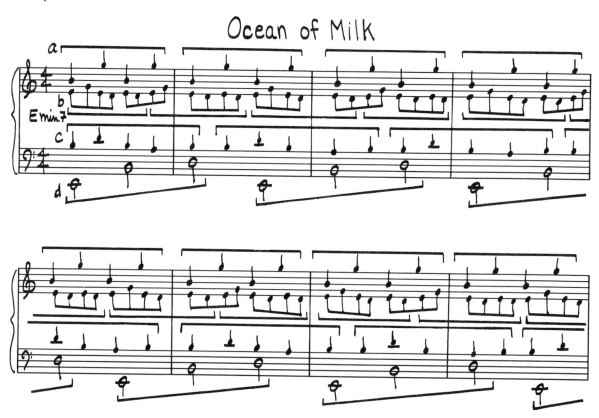

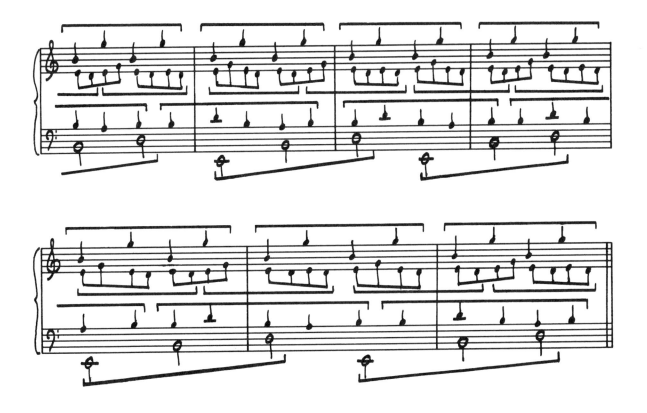

Exercise 16

1. Construct four ostinato patterns on a D min. 7 (D F A C) using only chord tones and Basic Note Values.

2. These patterns should be of the following lengths:

   a. three beats to be repeated twenty times
   b. two beats to be repeated thirty times
   c. four beats to be repeated fifteen times
   d. five beats to be repeated twelve times

   (If you do this correctly, all the patterns will begin anew on the sixty-first beat.)

3. Use separate manuscript paper for this exercise.

VOICE CROSSING

Another way of making more out of less is through *voice cross-ing.* In the repeated-tone accompaniment shown in Example L, *a,* instead of giving one instrument the upper tones and another the lower tones, you can alternate each instrument between the upper and lower tones, as shown in *b*. Even when played by two identical instruments (two trumpets, for example) *b* will sound different from *a*:

Example L

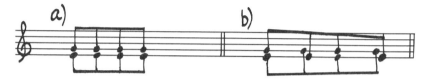

Exercise 17

Apply voice crossing to *a* employing two identical instruments or two instruments of similar range and weight (horn and trumpet, for example):

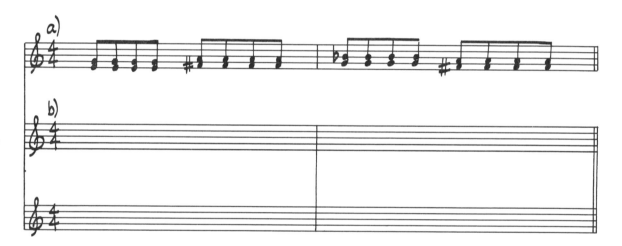

The voice-crossing process is an integral part of the gamelan music of Indonesia, in which it is often applied to more than two voices.

A further procedure derived from gamelan music is the distribution of a single melody among several instruments, each playing the entire melody, but in different tempos or rhythms. Example M uses a single three-note melody. Note the reiteration in the clarinet part. (It is possible to use more than one melody at a time. Also, you may want to investigate combining this gamelan procedure with voice crossing.)

214

Example M

Exercise 18

1. Compose a short melody (three or four tones long) based on tones of the D pentatonic scale.

2. Apply the procedure used in Example M and distribute the melody among five instruments.

Hint: This procedure is applicable to both melody and accompaniment.

AFTERTHOUGHTS

As I have said several times now, minimalism is a way of getting more out of less: for example, voice crossing, pointillism, heterophony, and so forth. Minimalism also suggests ways of keeping going, of spreading out material over a long stretch of time as seen in the ostinato (especially the modulating ostinato and the kaleidoscope ostinato). It is also minimalistic to derive chords from the melody (Chapter 9), construct a melody from the tones of organum (Chapter 13), and so forth.

But the essence of minimalism is limitation of resources as seen in the cell, the row, isorhythms, and the use of specific scales (major, Phrygian, Lixian, pentatonic, among others). Such a limitation of resources serves two purposes: first, it unifies the material, it holds the material together, and leads to the wholeness that all composers strive for; second, it acts as a stimulus to creativity. The reason why limitation of resources acts as a stimulus is not known, but it is undeniably true. Nothing is worse than sitting down to compose with the *limitlessness* of music stretching out before you. It is of great value to reduce this limitlessness, to know that you will compose a piece of three-minutes duration for flute and clarinet, using only the C Lixian scale and its transposition, such-and-such an isorhythm, and the small theme forms. With limitation of resources, you will feel safer, you will know what the limits of the task are, you will feel challenged, and you will want to make these meager materials into something of value.

Another supremely important aspect of minimalism is *stylistic*: for one thing, minimalism can lead you to avant-garde music or to popular music. How is minimalism avant-garde? The most obvious example would be in a melody drawn from the 12-tone row, with all harmonies derived from the melody. But you can compose avant-garde music even with a simple scale if you severely restrict all its elements. For example, you can compose a piece based on the pentatonic scale with two rhythms for pizzicato violin and muted trumpet used only as solo instruments or in organum with each other.

Minimalism also leads to popular music in ways almost too obvious to be listed, such as a small theme for flute based on the C pentatonic scale with an oom-pah accompaniment based on major and minor triads drawn from the C major scale.

My own interest in minimalism is that it can lead to what I call *populist* music, music that uses all the minimalistic procedures, but with more heart and passion than in avant-garde music, and more wit and wisdom than in popular music. At its worst, avant-garde distances itself from the audience, and popular music at its worst reaches out to its audience almost excessively, is too obvious and literal, and tells us nothing about the universe.

I hope that you are led to populism, if not now, perhaps sometime later. Regardless of how these ideas strike you, however, it is indisputable that you must find your own voice and obey it, and in this pursuit minimalism will be enormously helpful. Seek out the limitations and procedures that are most congenial, with which you are most at home, and that allow you to express the deepest part of your being.

Appendix A: Instrument Ranges

Here are the ranges of instruments you may be writing for in this book. The ranges are shown at actual pitch (except for the double bass, which always sounds an octave lower than written). This means that for some instruments you may have to consult the player you are writing for or an orchestration book for the correct transposition.

The range of each instrument is shown by open notes, and *practical* limits for most players are shown by black notes. (Individual players may have a wider or narrower range than shown, and you should always ask the players you are writing for about their particular abilities and limitations.)

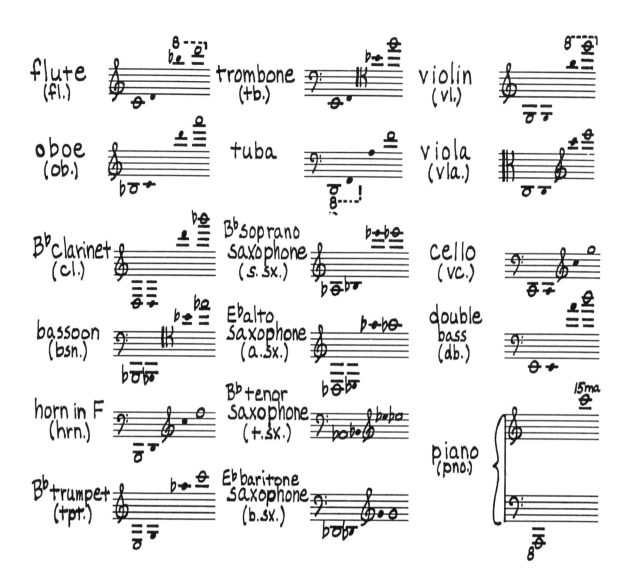

Appendix B:
Musical Symbols

Here are some useful symbols and their usual placement. These symbols are invaluable in helping a player make a piece come to life. In addition to using these symbols, you should indicate how a piece, or section of a piece, is to be performed ("sweetly," "sneakily," "dirge-like," and so on).

DYNAMICS

These are usually placed below the staff.

pp   *pianissimo* (very soft)

p   *piano* (soft)

mp   *mezzo-piano* (moderately soft)

mf   *mezzo-forte* (moderately loud)

f   *forte* (loud)

ff   *fortissimo* (very loud)

sfz   *sforzando* (suddenly loud)

fp   *forte-piano* (loud and immediately soft again)

cresc. (crescendo) gradually
increasing the volume

dim. (diminuendo) gradually
diminishing the volume

These may also be written as symbols:

(cresc.)

(dim.)

Note that dynamics are placed just *before* the first tone they affect.

ACCENTS

These are always placed outside the staff and near the head of the note.

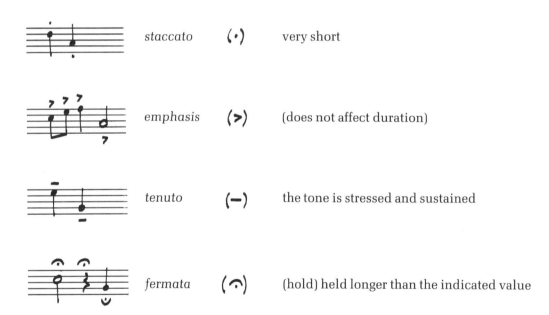

staccato (**·**) very short

emphasis (**>**) (does not affect duration)

tenuto (**–**) the tone is stressed and sustained

fermata (**⌒**) (hold) held longer than the indicated value

SLURS AND TIES

ties—placed above note heads when the stems are down and below note heads when the stems are up. The tones are held for the combined value of the notes involved. Only the first note is sounded.

ties—placed above whole notes that are on the third line or higher.

slurs—for a few notes and for short phrases, slurs are placed like ties when the stem direction for all notes is the same. The slur indicates that the notes involved are to be played *legato*—that is, smoothly or closely connected.

slurs—when one or more of the stems are down, slurs go above the notes.

TEMPO

These indications are generally written above the staff at the beginning of a piece and at any point where you want the tempo to change. Tempo may be indicated in two ways:

$\downarrow$=60

$\downarrow$=108, etc.

metronome marking—this symbol gives the tempo by telling you how many notes of the given value are in one minute.

caressingly, slow, a fast march

words—using words that describe the character and speed of the piece. You should consult a dictionary of musical terms and use your imagination for the many ways of explaining the character and mood you intend.

Here are some other terms you will find useful:

rit. (ritardando) gradually getting slower

accel. (accelerando) gradually getting faster; this is usually followed by a change in tempo, or *a tempo* (return to the original tempo)

GENERAL SYMBOLS

﹐ = *breath mark* (this also suggests a pause for non-wind instruments)

tr. = *trill*

tr.⌒⌒ = *trill* (for ½ notes or longer)

sim. (simile) similarly; continue a formula that has been indicated, such as an accent pattern or the arpeggiating of chords (*simile* may be placed above or below the staff)

Appendix C:
Bibliography

Apel, Willi. *Harvard Dictionary of Music.* Cambridge, Mass.: Harvard University Press, 1970.

Dallin, Leon. *Techniques of Twentieth Century Composition.* Dubuque, Iowa: Wm. C. Brown Publishers, 1974.

Engel, Lehman. *Their Words Are Music.* 1975.

————. *Words with Music.* New York: Schirmer Books, 1972.

Gershwin, Ira. *Lyrics on Several Occasions.* New York: Alfred A. Knopf, 1959.

Hindemith, Paul. *The Craft of Musical Composition.* 2 vols. New York: Associated Music Publishers, 1941.

Johnson, Roger. *Scores: An Anthology of New Music.* New York: Schirmer Books, 1981.

Jones, George Thaddeus. *Music Composition.* Evanston, Ill.: Summy-Birchard, 1963.

Kennan, Kent Wheeler. *The Technique of Orchestration.* Englewood Cliffs, N.J.: Prentice-Hall, Inc., 1970.

McKay, George Frederick. *Creative Orchestration.* Boston: Allyn and Bacon, 1963.

Persichetti, Vincent. *Twentieth-Century Harmony: Creative Aspects and Practice.* New York: W. W. Norton, 1961.

Piston, Walter. *Orchestration.* New York: W. W. Norton, 1955.

Russo, William. *Composing for the Jazz Orchestra.* Chicago: University of Chicago Press, 1961.

————. *Jazz Composition and Orchestration.* Chicago: University of Chicago Press, 1968.

Index